Bakery Face

Story of a Second Chance

Scott T. Sammis & Tina M. Sammis

Contents

CHAPTER 1. The Interview

It had been a rough three years, coming into the third winter since my wife Mary died suddenly. I felt tired and was losing faith. It was December 8, 2008. Mary had passed away 35 months and 2 days ago. Today was my daughter Becky's 26th birthday, son John would be 24 in 11 days, and Trevor 28 in 27 days, January 4th, the day Mary died. We were all in a slow recovery from the body blow of losing her suddenly to a rock slide on Mount Kilimanjaro. After selling the family insurance business the next year, I was in the final year of my earn out contract and 100% absorbed in running the company as its president. My partner Frank and I had a challenging job open in our business insurance department. A promising candidate was coming to interview at 6pm. that evening.

Our offices in Woodbury, Long Island were impressive. The lobby was framed by ionic columns, over-arched by a lighted dome, and touched classically by wood paneling, a chandelier and a round glass table with a large floral arrangement. The holiday spirit was enhanced by a row of poinsettias lining the long hallway reaching to the back of the office. Leather couches beckoned customers and guests to be comfortable while they waited.

A little before 6pm I heard the front lobby doorbell chime, and someone let the candidate in. Frank and I believed in team interviews. He had met her already and invited her back for a second interview, a positive sign. He had questions about her long and colorful resume, but felt she could fit in well with our company. In his words, she was "our kind of people," hardworking, smart, loyal and a team player. I reviewed her resume, noted the many stops along the way, and prepared a few questions. In 25 years I had interviewed hundreds of candidates. I didn't expect any surprises. To create the exceptional staff we had assembled, Frank and I needed to be very selective. Hiring mistakes always turned out costly and painful. I was already thinking beyond the interview to dinner at home by myself – Becky was celebrating her birthday with friends – as I walked from my office to greet the newcomer. What happened next took my breath away and changed my life.

There she was! I couldn't believe my eyes! Of course she was gorgeous, in her form-fitting black pinstripe suit with a red top and heels. But it was her face, her eyes, her hair framing them. Her face was so open and radiant with promise and acceptance. Her eyes, black as coal and bright, shining with wisdom, mischief and curiosity. Her straight velvety black hair caressed her face and captivated me. My heart leaped up into my throat. I was stunned, weak-kneed, heart fluttering, but at the same time absolutely certain I had just laid eyes on The One. Normally fairly formal, I shook her hand and said "I'm Scott, welcome," but then I pulled her in for a brief greeting hug. She was taken aback, but kept her composure and smiled happily. "Thanks," she said, "I'm Tina."

I barely remember the interview itself. My mind was racing, made up: we were hiring her, no matter what. I didn't get to ask my questions, as Frank and the others did a good job grilling her. I just stared at Tina, trying not to be too obvious, not believing that the woman I had been searching for had just found me. Could it be true? Were my prayers being answered? Was this really happening? I honestly did not know if Tina was married – we were forbidden from asking – but it didn't matter. I knew once she became part of our team, most likely she would be with the company a long time, as most of our employees were. In the fullness of time, I would have my chance....wow, wow, WOW.

December 8th, 2008. The Great Recession has just begun. Lehman Brothers crashed and the insurance agency I was working for as a lead Marketing Representative realized they were in trouble. The last 30 new hires were to be let go; and I was one of them. I was panicked. At 44 years old, I was the breadwinner of my family of two, and I had never been let go from a job before. I was always the one leaving for a better opportunity. This was a foreign feeling for me. I hated it.

The interviewing process had started. As I drove up to my 2nd interview at 125 Froehlich Farm Boulevard in

Woodbury, NY, I already had two job offers, but I sensed they were not the right fit for me. My husband James advised "take one of these jobs, you may not be worth all you think you are." His words infuriated me, but they were not unusual, unfortunately. I suspected all along that as I became more successful, he became more resentful, insecure, and jealous. I was feeling defiant and confident as I walked through the doors for a 2nd time. I wore my best interview suit, black with light blue pin stripes and an red silk top.

The receptionist Denise let me in - she wasn't the friendliest and it almost seemed like she was feeling put upon - but I didn't care. I had been advised by the head hunter that the 2nd interview would be with the namesake of Sammis Insurance Agency, Scott Sammis. Tom, the head hunter, advised me that Scott was a Harvard and Brown graduate, extremely smart, but very down to earth. All I heard was "Harvard and Brown graduate," and I couldn't imagine that Harvard and Brown went along with down to earth.

As I sat in the beautifully holiday decorated foyer for what felt like an hour (in actuality it was five minutes), out came the very handsome, very tall Mr. Scott Sammis. He greeted me with a wide smile. I stood up from the couch and extended my hand to greet him, but he pulled me in for a brief hug. Hmmm, was that normal? A move like that from a prospective employer would normally have sent me walking *right out the door. Oddly enough if felt warm and natural.*

The interview was a formality, in my mind at least. We were hiring this amazing, radiant woman. There were a few obstacles, however. First, she was obviously abundantly employable, a real catch, because she had two job offers already, in a frightful job market. Would she take the job? Second, her resume was colorful, full of many steps up the ladder. You had to admire her ambition and drive, but she seemed to change jobs like others change clothes. I'd had only 3 jobs with 2 companies in 25+ years. As he always did, Frank finished up the second interview with Tina with a question: "Is there any reason you couldn't see yourself staying with our company for 10 years?" Tina, despite the litany of job changes, enthusiastically said "No!" Third, the assignment we had for her was problematic. She would be replacing the current leader of a four person team, who would be demoted but remain with the team, and leading three other semi-disgruntled team members. We fully explained this mess, she accepted the challenge, and I knew she could do it. But did *she?*

I took the job! The pay was was a little less than the other offers and what I normally would accept, but times were tough, companies weren't hiring like normal, they were laying off, and I was intrigued to see what this opportunity would bring. My husband James gave me his usual back handed compliment, meant to keep me just a little below him.

My sister Tonianne, my confidante, advised me "you are worth more. Don't take that job." I was too afraid to take her advice this time. She later was thrilled I didn't take her advice.

CHAPTER 2. Working Together

2009 started auspiciously for me. Business conditions were awful, but Tina was on board the mother ship. As thrilled as I was to see her every day, I felt no urgency to reveal my feelings to anyone or press our relationship. After all, I "knew" she'd be with us for 10 years. She said so. Plenty of time. I grew complacent. Which didn't mean I missed any opportunity to cruise by her office - Harvard Business School had taught me the utility of MBWA, "managing by walking around" - or pretend not to gaze at her in meetings, or "happen" to follow her into the kitchen for a cup of coffee. I plead guilty to all charges. I supposed no one noticed. But I had a serious crush on the new girl, permanently, unavoidably smitten. She was gracious, but gave no indication of interest. Over time, I learned a little of her marriage. She didn't offer much. Occasionally she was tearful, with others, and I guessed it might be marriage-related. I could only hope.

We had sold the business to USI, a national insurance broker (the initials don't stand for anything) on January 3, 2007, 364 days after Mary died. 2009 was my final contract year. USI had led me to believe my job would be devoted to growing the practice, acquiring new agencies, managing the melding together of disparate cultures, looking for larger space, etc. Perfect for me, I thought. I spent the first five months of my contract doing just that, dreaming of new horizons to conquer. Not so fast. In May USI sold itself to Goldman Sachs Private Equity Partners, and the game changed. I knew the new business imperative. In order to afford the interest payments on the mountain of debt GSPEP had taken on to buy USI, expenses in our company would need to be slashed. Goldman was relentless in the pursuit of profit, so the growth dreams died suddenly and violently, and the process of laying off three quarters of the staff I'd built over 25 years began. Eight were ushered out of their workplaces with cardboard boxes by USI Human Resources staff that first summer. A dozen more followed each year thereafter. I fought, argued, resisted and lost. Incredibly, the loss of accounts that I predicted turned out to be minimal, even as the blood-letting continued. Heartbreaking. Confusing.

I came to work on that Monday in December, knowing about some of the obstacles. Scott and his partner Frank had been honest that this job had real challenges, and they were right. I was hired to be the team leader of a dysfunctional unit. I would be replacing the current team leader, who would then be asked to work under me. In the first few weeks I called team meetings. My team was distant and distracted, offering no help with how the office procedures and systems worked. It was clear I would have to win them over. Surprisingly enough, the woman I replaced stepped up and realized we needed to pull together or we would all sink together. She helped acclimate me, giving me the tools I needed to become the leader I knew I could be. The others started to come around.

The pressing demand for more analysis, reports and crisis updates by my new overlords at GS/USI wore me out. Instead of growing our company, I was feeding the voracious profit/layoff machine. My final year was shaping up to be a soul-crushing grind. I had crafted my exit plan. I just needed to survive the 12 months. A necessary part of my plan for the ultimate year was to not reveal a secret, for which I believed I might be fired, thus voiding my contract: I was seeing a divorced fellow employee around my age. We both agreed USI might not look kindly on the relationship, and she agreed to keep our arrangement to ourselves, especially never telling her gossipy sister, who also worked at the company, and happened to be a member of Tina's team. I was confident no one would ever know...

Of course I knew. As I gained my team's trust, I got an earful of office gossip. The handsome Scott Sammis, with the piercing blue eyes, had suffered a tragic loss. The Sammis family, in January 2006 took a once in a lifetime trip to Mount Kilimanjaro in Africa to climb this beast of a mountain. There was a rock slide, and Scott's beloved wife and mother of his three children was struck by a rock. The rock punctured her lung, and she passed away on the mountain. I was terribly upset for him and his family. I also learned that he had recently started to date one of the divorced ladies in our office, who happened to be the sister of one of my most difficult teammates. I was shocked on both fronts. I felt sadness for his loss, and bewildered by his choice of mates.

I was also surprised of a feeling budding within me. One day around the water cooler, one of the attractive available female sales reps had mentioned to me while Scott was getting out of his Mustang, "now that's my kind of guy." I felt an immediate pang of jealousy. "What the hell was that feeling about?" I asked myself. I hadn't felt that emotion in many years. And I wasn't supposed to. I was married!

As frustrated, nervous and worn out as I was during the first half of 2009, I was coming out of my complacency with Tina. Over time I was excruciatingly torn by my inability to get closer to her. I knew we would eventually be together, but I couldn't wait for some progress, any progress. I needed to open my heart to her, to hear her story. All apparently impossible. She was a model employee, successfully knitting the troubled team into a coherent, efficient, bonded unit. She was unflaggingly positive, cheerful, and respected by all. I could tell a few of the single gentlemen in the office were interested. But she wasn't. She was married, loyal, and simply not able to entertain another possibility. I deeply respected that. But it was frustrating as hell. I consoled myself with the "knowledge" that I had all the time in the world. Right.

Tina and I shared occasional email conversations about business. Everyone in the office figured the company email was monitored by GS/USI, so caution was an imperative. Just before her planned vacation in June, an annual Sisters Weekend in California, my caution wavered. She mentioned the getaway in an innocent email, and I responded "can you fit me in your suitcase?" and hit SEND before my better instincts could kick in. I don't know what came over me. My better angel said "what have you just done?", but a hopeful smile crossed my face, nonetheless.

Before thinking, I immediately responded to the email, "Yes, but you may be too tall to fit." Scott, in that email, just became human to me. I felt guilty but enthralled. What does this mean?

I had a little secret of my own. Two previous business associates, involved in a long process of setting up a new commercial lines shop in a competing construction insurance agency, had been calling me every week since I started at Sammis. No one knew besides me. They were offering me $25,000 more than I was making here. I was torn and guilty, but I knew what I had to do. I was not happy to leave. I was finally feeling at home at 125 Froehlich Farm Boulevard.

Flush with optimism about this unexpected barrier-breaking email exchange, I was completely unprepared for what happened next. Just before she left for the Sisters Weekend, Tina called Frank and me and asked for a meeting. She didn't let on what it was about, but my heart sank. This couldn't be good. True to form, Tina joined us to announce she had received a job offer she couldn't refuse. She looked sheepish and apologetic, and she convinced us she really did love working with us. However, the offer was $25,000 higher than we were paying. Because of the tight budget constraints imposed by GS/USI we couldn't even offer $25 more, let alone a meaningful counter offer. I was bereft, crestfallen, crushed by the news. How could this be? What about my nine and a half more years? She looked sad, but determined. There was nothing else left to say.

I walked her out of my office and down the long, columned hallway - the cheerful holiday poinsettias were long gone. Midway back to her office, I had an idea, and I stopped her. "Let me have your cell phone number, so we can stay in touch." The lump in my throat made it difficult to croak out the request. "Here, write it on the back of my business card." She smiled and scribbled the numbers on the card. We parted. By the time she reached her office, her cell was ringing. It was me. You know how women will sometimes transpose a pair of digits in a phone number, just to throw a guy off the scent? I needed to know this number was legitimate. She answered, surprised it was me. I said "Sorry, just checking. Have a great vacation." I had a feeling this wasn't the end...

CHAPTER 3. The Lunches

Here I am in my new big office with my new construction insurance team and my $25000 increase. My sister is proud, my husband humbled. I just got the biggest job in my career in the middle of a terrible economic contraction. I was excited about the new challenges that awaited me. My new clients were multimillion dollar construction firms, and I was the only woman allowed in the boys club. I felt pretty empowered. By the way, fantasy football was ramping up, and I was in the competition. To the boys' chagrin, I won the whole enchilada that year!

I was not expecting to hear from Scott. I figured he might call someday. Before I left his firm a month ago, he had asked me for my cell phone number. I wasn't in the habit of giving my number to other men, but my heart needed to stay in touch....

In her beautiful new office at her new job, Tina heard her cell phone ring. She had enough self-accountability that she could afford to pick up the personal call. It was me. She seemed surprised to hear my voice, but pleased, I thought. "Remember when I got your number in the hallway and said we needed to stay in touch? Well, it's me." Not mentioning a purpose or proposal, I merely asked if she could schedule a lunch sometime in the next few weeks.

Well, look who called? A lunch? I thought, why not? I was assuming a counter offer was in store. In my past experience of leaving companies, there had been instances where the bosses would "find money in the budget" and try to lure me back. I was looking forward to seeing Scott's face and negotiating. I thought his partner Frank might come also. "How about 7ᵗʰ Street Cafe in Garden City next Friday?"

I left the USI office that next Friday, a man on a mission, but one who needed to proceed with extreme caution. I couldn't stop thinking about Tina after she left our company. I desperately wanted to preserve whatever flickering hope of a future relationship there might be. I knew she was loyal to her marriage, and that, if I pushed the issue, I could easily blow it. I needed only to express my honest feelings and hope she didn't faint, become offended, or run out of the restaurant screaming. On the drive to Garden City I resolved my goal would be limited: just secure one more lunch.

The 7ᵗʰ Street Cafe in GC is an upscale white linen restaurant. That day it was about one half full with patrons when I arrived early. I was seated when I saw Tina come

7th Street Cafe

in the door. She wore a green and white floral sun dress a

touch above the knee. I'd forgotten how beautiful she was. My palms started to sweat. She spied me, smiled and joined me at the corner table. I arose, gave her another gentle embrace, and settled her chair. Ever chivalrous.

We chatted about her new job and her co-workers in the USI Sammis crew, but I soon began to feel she was waiting for me to play my hand. Here goes, I gulped to myself. "You probably know why I asked you to lunch today?" I offered. Tina looked nonplussed. "Is it about a counter offer?" Uh oh, I thought, I didn't see that one coming. Press on, this is important. "No," I admitted. I watched as a little doubt ran across Tina's face. "I think you're wonderful. I know you're married, and I don't want to upset or pressure you in any way. I just know in my heart we would be spectacular together." Tina's eyes widened, and there was a barely perceptible intake of breath, but nothing escaped her mouth. The good news was she didn't spit out her club soda or run out of the restaurant. She was clearly stunned, but her eyes said "I'm listening."

I pressed on, feeling a little wave of confidence. So far, so good. Neither of us had touched our salads, her dressing on the side was still sitting there, waiting patiently. Time for a little more honesty. "I have very strong feelings for you, and can clearly see a long storybook relationship. All I really want is a 40 year honeymoon with you." Her mouth fell open even wider. No stroke or vomit. Time to soften. "I respect your marriage vows. Your loyalty makes me want you more. Here's what I have to offer: I will wait TEN YEARS for you. Not eleven, but not nine either. Ten years. You are that important to me. I just know that if I didn't tell you these things, I would kick myself for the whole rest of my life."

W T F ??? What just happened? This man I admired and wondered about was confessing to me his intense feelings. Was I secretly hoping for this confession? At that moment, I could not say. I can tell you that I was honored. I know that sounds like a strange way to describe his exchange, but at the moment honored was what I felt. I still couldn't speak, let alone touch my food. I had a feeling I didn't need to say anything, but he had more to say.

I was giddy, having gotten out my message, avoided having to hate myself for eternity, and played my cards. The ball was in my lovely Tina's court, and heart. I had to ask one more thing, as we gazed at each other over still uneaten salads and puddling dressing on the side. "For now, I need no response, no reaction. I know I've thrown you for a loop. My only request is, will you have one more lunch with me, maybe in a month?" One heart beat, another, and she smiled. "Of course. Call me." Yippee! I'm still alive to fight another day. That was NOT a NO!

CHAPTER 4. Tina's Dilemna

I left the 7th Street Cafe in a fog. I felt lightheaded and wanted to tell someone what had just happened. I wanted to make it real. But of course that was impossible. I was married and loyal. I come from a large and close knit Italian family that believes in making things work. Although, truth be told, my family did not have the same feelings toward my husband as I did. It wasn't for lack of trying. Attempting always to "make it work," they tried to welcome Jim, but were met with resistance and coldness. My marriage was missing important components for survival.

When I saw my husband that evening I felt guilt stricken. Without knowing it, Scott's proposal forced me into a painful comparison of where I was and where I wanted to be. The aspects of a relationship that I found so simple, like having a Sunday dinner with the loved ones, exploring new places, and the best thing, having children, were difficult with Jim.

My husband James came from a dysfuctional household as an only child. He was adopted at birth by a loveless and frightened couple. When he located and attempted to contact his maternal mother, she hung up the phone. James tried to give me all he could. But he was unexamined. After 5 years of marriage, he was turning a corner we could not survive. I felt isolated from my family by his reluctance to spend time with them. He was jealous of my time with friends and others, dismissive of my accomplishments. I entered the marriage hoping for children. He changed his mind. When he became more verbally abusive, I knew we were in trouble.

I found myself fantasizing about a life with Scott. At that point, Jim and I had been to counseling a dozen times. After fights I used the words "I'm DONE!" way too much. Jim would respond and try to make things better. A week after my first lunch with Scott, Jim and I were walking in New York City. I was still on Cloud Nine from the experience. Jim opened up to me with tears that I was the only person in his life that mattered. I immediately stopped fantasizing. At least I tried. I thought to myself, a second lunch with Scott would not be the right thing to do.

I knew the lunch at 7th Street Cafe had created a crisis in Tina's mind, a firestorm of conscience. I could sense she yearned for a honeymoon also, but her intense loyalty and tenacity would make her want to call us off. I could only pray that, in a moment of weakness or hope or self-discovery she would allow one more lunch. I screwed up my courage and called...

I had decided to decline Scott's next lunch invitation. Jim had poured out his heart on our walk in NYC and seemed to be really trying. I didn't want to hurt him, he needed me. As much as I wanted to have lunch to see Scott and enjoy his smile and our conversations, it felt a little wrong. Truthfully, smiles and fun conversations were rare for Jim and me at this point.

Scott confused me. As urgent as his plea was, his attitude was incredibly patient. He planted his seed and let it grow naturally. Looking back, had he pushed harder, this wouldn't have worked. I began to wonder if he had forgotten me. It had been what seemed like months since our lunch, and I hadn't heard from him. I was prepared to gently decline a second lunch. It was the right thing to do.

Then the phone rang, and I heard that voice, so hopeful, happy and full of promise. Before I could even think about it, "Yes!" came out of my mouth. We were on for one more lunch.

B K Sweeney's in Garden City is more of a pub atmosphere than the 7th Street Cafe, wooden booths and lower lighting. We met on another Friday, this time in the fall. We didn't eat another fine meal together again. All I know is I felt euphoric - I was still ALIVE! Part of me was amazed she had said yes. I didn't want to ask too many questions about that decision. Didn't want to blow my chance.

B K Sweeney's

Parking in Garden City at lunch time is a nightmare. After driving around madly searching for a spot, we finally met outside, entered the pub and found a booth. This time, we both talked.

I guess I let her get a few words in. Her voice was music to my ears. What she talked about I have no idea, I was so smitten, so gaga. I was listening with my eyes and heart, not my ears. Then she said something that brought me up short.

"I'm feeling a little guilty," she said a little timidly. "If my husband was having lunch with someone he was attracted to, I don't know that I would like it much." I almost jumped out of my seat and started dancing on the table. They would still be talking about it at B K Sweeney's if I had. My heart leaped out of my chest instead. All I heard was "attracted to," which to this day I still interpret as "had feelings for." SHE HAS FEELINGS FOR ME!!! WOW! I was miles ahead of Tina, but she was inching toward me. That was entirely good enough for me.

Our second lunch was much more casual and comfortable. We met at a pub in Garden City, always close to my office, and again did not eat a bite. We talked and talked. I loved our conversations, so hopeful and positive. He asked me about my dreams, and places I wanted to travel to, things I hadn't thought about for years. When I think back on those times, I had been holding in so much of my excitement and wonder. Dreams were not in my daily life. It was work, obligation and practical decisions. Quite a bit of compromise and sacrifice were more the reality than dreams. When Scott asked about my dreams for the future, the only thing that came to mind was to "save abandoned kittens." He must have thought I'd be a crazy cat lady! I just couldn't imagine beyond that.

I told Scott I felt guilty and was attracted to him. I didn't want to lead him on, but I just couldn't lie to him.

I was euphoric about the revelation of Tina's feelings, so I asked right then and there for another lunch. She didn't hesitate. We left each other saying "can't wait," with a polite hug, no kiss.

I thought of Tina constantly that fall of 2009, but my attention was drawn inexorably to the final two months of my three year contract. Not only was I counting the days, but the agency's revenue was lagging behind our commitments. Large penalties loomed. My lunches with Tina were a welcome respite of hope and life.

Leo's

Our third lunch was in December at the famous Garden City burger joint, Leo's.

As our chances together grew brighter and upgraded, at least in my mind, we moved downscale in our lunch venues. No matter, we hardly ate anyway. Since B K Sweeney's Tina and I had talked a few times on the telephone. Mostly she spoke about her beloved, ailing best cat buddy Jake. I love cats, and Tina had the makings of a cat lady, so I felt we bonded. The familiar chit chat was warmer now, more natural. We shared our feelings in the burger joint. We also shared a holiday cocktail. Maybe it was the wine talking, or the holiday spirit, but towards the end of the hour, Tina smiled coquettishly and said "after Christmas, let's get together and have dinner or drinks, so we don't have to rush."

Boom, there went my heart again. I felt like dancing in the end zone after a spectacular touchdown! Was she suggesting a new level??? I thought so. Now I COULD NOT WAIT for the holidays to be over. What a happy new year 2010 was promising to be....

By Christmas time things were pretty rocky once again with my husband. James' contracting business would go through periods of drought. During those times his moods would darken, and our conversations would turn to blame and accusations. I would try to get him to promote his business and think of alternative ways to make money. He, in turn, found my suggestions to be controlling and preachy. These times were becoming more and more frequent. Coupled with the stress of James being reluctantly around my family, the holidays were turning into a nightmare for me. To top it off, I found out later he was knee deep in an affair with our real estate agent's wife.

Scott called for our holiday lunch. This time there was no hesitation on my part, no second guessing. I think I was preparing for a change. We went to a local Garden City pub called Leo's. We had a drink, and the hour flew by. I suggested our next meeting should be dinner or drinks after work. He didn't know it, but I wanted to kiss him. At that point, I had a feeling of new beginnings- a way out.

CHAPTER 5. Guess What?

My upcoming rendezvous with Tina was foremost in my mind during Christmas '09 and New Years '10. My three children and I trekked to Northern California for our annual holiday reunion with Mary's extended family. A warm, fun time, this year it was mostly delightful because I got to spend more time than usual with my three favorite people on the planet: Trevor, Becky and John. Since Mary passed, these trips always had a tinge of loneliness for me. This year I was going back East to finish up my time with GSPE/USI, and say goodbye to the wonderful staff that had survived the layoff grim reaper. But I would be saying hello to a brand new life-changing 40 year honeymoon with Tina. I hoped.

For years I wanted a home filled with children. In the early part of our marriage Jim and I had agreed to this vision. However, fate had other ideas. Jim's experience with fathering a child with his ex-girlfriend, and dealing with her hostile manipulations, made him increasingly bitter and resentful. In time he changed his mind about having children with me. My family dream got crushed. For a few years I clung to the belief that time would change Jim's mind.

In our early marriage years we power saved and bought - and paid off - a vacation condo in Florida. We always wanted a cute home on Long Island. Our real estate feelers were out constantly. We found a real estate agent scouting for us, and periodically we would look at houses. They never seemed to be quite right: too big, too much work required, too expensive. In early January 2010 Jim came home with the exciting news that he had found the perfect home for us. It was, he added "a home that either one of us could afford if our marriage didn't work out." Huh, I thought, pausing to let that statement sink in. In the context of finally achieving our home dream, this wasn't a reassuring or typical idea.

Oddly, on some level, I was OK with it. When he took me to see the house, he was right, it was a keeper. Brightly colored rooms filled with light,

312 S. 5th Street, Lindenhurst

beautifully appointed, ready to move in. I could definitely envision myself living there. The couple selling were going through a nasty divorce, and the bank had it as a short sale. We decided to go for it. We told our broker "we're in!" I was thinking of decorating and feathering my new nest. A long held dream was about to come true. One thing I wasn't thinking about was Scott.

The day came for me to call Tina and set up our relationship-launching "date." It was a bright, shining, cold January day, and I was feeling energized. My three year contract was complete, and we had achieved our revenue commitment by a whisker, so there would be not penalties. There seemed to be a light at the end of my rough, four year tunnel. And my love train with Tina seemed ready to leave the station. All aboard!

Her voice on the phone was warm. And excited. I asked her how the holidays were for her. She said she had news! Jim and she were buying a home together! I felt all the air rush out of my lungs, and my heart sank. I probably muttered something like "oh, that's so great," but I knew it was the collapse of a dream for me. I knew that when couples found themselves in marital trouble, they would often resort to grasping at straws, sometimes serious ones. They might get a puppy, become pregnant, or...buy a house. Tina sounded truly jubilant as she described the house - cute, welcoming, totally finished, perfect for her. I could say I felt happy for her, but truly I was desperately sad for me, and for us. I "forgot" to ask her for our date, making excuses for how busy I was wrapping up all the details of the business contract. I said I would call in a few weeks. I knew I wouldn't. What about the ten years? Yeah, right. A gloom settled over me....

I noticed a couple weeks after I told Scott about the house, he hadn't called. I was consumed with all that goes into purchasing a home. The first few weeks after our decision to pursue the dream South Street home, Jim and I were like newlyweds, looking at furniture, envisioning cooking and entertaining. I couldn't wait to have family visit, and maybe stay over.

February came, and things turned sour. The bank was obnoxiously nit picky. We had excellent credit, no debt, and plenty of cash to put down, but the lender managed to come up with a never-ending supply of obstacles.

By March, Jim was out late on Friday nights and would not tell me where he'd been. I would ask if he was seeing someone, and his stock answer was "it's not about that." My sisters were convinced he was cheating, and were protective of me. Although I felt hurt and uncertain, there was no panic. I also felt relief, and enjoyed my time alone for some much needed soul searching on my quiet Friday nights. I was starting to envision myself in my dream home alone.

I absorbed the emotional blow about Tina and threw myself into my impending retirement. What else could I do? The Tina dream door seemed shut tight. I supposed the house might fall through, and I had promised to wait ten years, after all. I placed our relationship in a compartment in my mind. The door to the that little room opened frequently, I smiled, sighed, and closed the door. There were pressing matters to worry about.

GS/USI was up to its usual skullduggery. Any lingering thoughts I had entertained of extending my Presidency evaporated. I hated the idea of abandoning my loyal staff – many of whom I had known for 10 plus years – and felt guilty about getting out. USI smashed those misgivings. On Valentine's Day, the Regional HR Director called to inform me that another five layoffs would occur April 1st, including the woman I had been seeing. These were all goodhearted, loyal, hardworking souls who had done nothing wrong. But USI needed its "margin." The Regional Executive also let me know he had reallocated the bonus pool, our Long Island branch had earned through sweat and sacrifice in 2009, to other branches, including the one he was domiciled in. His group had turned in a poor profit performance, and he felt bad. I was livid, and said so loudly and publicly. He eventually relented - we got half the pool we were entitled to. My mind was made up. I'd seen enough.

I chose April 10th as a retirement date, just before my 58th birthday. USI threw me a company party at a nearby restaurant, and my family organized another for friends, neighbors and closest company pals at my house on April 25th. A huge chapter in my life was over. Lillian, one of our most loyal survivors, happened to see Tina at Macy's just before the retirement party at the house and told me "she looks wonderful." I made a mental note to call her, just to see how her dream house was going.

About this time my children decided I needed an intervention. I had been moping about being scared of retiring, the end of my working career, having lost Tina. Once or twice I whined something like this to them: "you know, I've been thinking. I had a wonderful marriage of 30 years with your mom, my soul mate. I feel very fortunate and blessed to have had those years. I feel greedy even hoping for a second soul mate. I probably should settle now for a comfortable relationship, you know even-keeled, low drama. After all, one soul mate per lifetime is pretty great, right? It's all one has a right to ask for."

The kids took me to a sunset beach in Centerport after the retirement party, poured me my favorite rum and coke, and said, ominously, "Dad, we have to talk." Uh oh, I worried. Lay it on me. "We hear you talk about settling, cashing in on your dreams for a special relationship. We have one word for that idea: BULLSHIT! You have taught us to keep seeking, pushing, never settling, and we're not about to let YOU off the hook. You will keep on pursuing your dream. What's happening with Tina?" I burst into tears, so proud I was of them. I remembered Lillian's words. It was time to keep pursuing those dreams, come hell or high water. I called Tina.

Scott called from out of the blue in mid-May. My heart skipped a beat. It had been dormant and aching for some time. I figured maybe Scott had forgotten his promise to wait the ten years. I don't know what made him call at this time. The romantic in me wanted to call it fate. My family insisted it was an intervention from above, most likely my mom. I later learned it was Lillian who put the bug in Scott's ear.

Ruth's Chris Steakhouse

In any event, we met for our fourth and final "lunch" at Ruth's Chris Steakhouse in Garden City. Once again very little food was consumed as our mouths were busy catching up on our months apart. I realized if these lunches became a habit, we'd both soon suffer from malnutrition, but we'd die happy. Was I ready again to take this relationship to the next level?

Scott told me about the sale of his business, and the expectations he had for the future. He informed me that when we got married ,it would not be at an all-inclusive Sandals. He knew that's where Jim and I had been married, and it haunted me that my family could not come to my wedding, and my dad couldn't walk me down the aisle. I smiled through a tear. What confidence this guy had!

By the end of May our dream house fell through, finally and utterly. The bank was asking for an additional $50,000, which was the last nail in the coffin of our home dream. At this point, James and I were merely roommates, just going *through the motions. The plan to purchase the cute South 5th Street house could not have fallen through at a better time. I have come to believe it was a blessing from my mom, Antoinette DeSantis.*

Now it's early May 2010. My disengagement from a 32 working career was complete. All the advisers and retirement gurus insisted that retirement NOT be approached without a PLAN. I had no plan, except to undertake a long held dream: a cross country Harley Davidson motorcycle trip. After my mom died in early 1998 I experienced a mid-life bucket list moment and bought a starter 650cc Yamaha V star classic, because it looked like a Harley. I learned to ride on that bike, and then my son Trevor took a nasty spill on it in the summer of 2002. He broke an ankle and both wrists. Getting the call that our oldest son was in the intensive care unit at Stony Brook University Hospital was one of the worst moments of my life. Mary forbid me from buying another motorcycle. The next year I couldn't wait so I bought a 2003 100th Anniversary Harley Soft tail classic 1500cc 800lb. beast and beauty. I could not stop fantasizing about a ride down to Florida or across to California. After I "lost" Tina to her dream house, I planned the cross country venture with my lady friend from work. I was retired, she was divorced and laid off, and a huge Harley aficionado. She had the same size motorcycle as me and had been across the continent once already with a big group. I was excited for the one month journey.

I called Tina not knowing what to expect, but encouraged by my kids and curious from Lillian's comment. I didn't want to let myself get overly hopeful, so I approached cautiously. She answered her cellphone warmly, enthusiastically and receptively. Hope started to stir, but only a little. She agreed quickly to meet at Ruth's Chris Steakhouse in Garden City for lunch. It certainly wasn't the drinks/dinner and possible kisses I had set my heart on in January, but it still seemed like magic to me. We picked up right where we left off, talking excitedly, listening intently, getting lost in each others eyes, and not eating, as usual. She showed a new frustration with her situation, and a confidence and bravado. Her fear had ebbed, and her determination was surfacing. She wouldn't be specific, but I knew things had changed. Maybe I wouldn't have to wait almost 9 years? We parted promising to get together soon, in the next few weeks. I didn't really know what to expect, but it felt very promising. All, that is, except me having to explain the motorcycle trip with another woman.

By early June the South Street home that was going to save my marriage to Jim completely fell through. The bankers won out. Jim had not confessed to his affair, but to me it was obvious. The signs were all there. My sisters were right. I was planning to move into a summer rental in Long Beach. Amazingly, Jim was trying to convince me to stay in our apartment and live as friends. His fantasy was we would play out our current dramas, and "find our way back to each other." He wanted to have his affair and have me waiting at home for when he was through. He wanted his cake and to eat it too. It seemed bizarre and delusional to me.

Serendipitously I was browsing in a hardware store in Babylon and came across a plaque that stated "If your ship doesn't come in, Swim out to it." I felt immediately that plaque was a sign from my mom up above telling me it was my time to swim. I emailed Scott that evening. The title line was Remember Me?

A Sign from Mom

CHAPTER 6. Remember Me?

How thrilled was I to get that email? Tina was taking initiative, jumping on board. I felt bowled over. Best email, EVER. I was filled to overflowing with optimism and promise. There was, of course, a problem. I was days away from beginning that long-dreamed of motorcycle journey across America with my laid off lady friend. No matter, I decided. I wrote back to Tina immediately, slightly embarrassed about the upcoming trip. I sheepishly explained I would be gone for four weeks, on the adventure with my friend from work, but enthusiastically suggested a dinner the minute I returned in mid-July. I proffered a few dates. She came back instantly with any Friday night at the end of July, and asked Where? I was giddy by now, so I replied "Hawaii?" I guess I was fast forwarding to our 40 year honeymoon. She seemed delighted by that idea, but we agreed on Fat Fish, a waterfront wine and fish spot in Bayshore, that first Friday after I got off

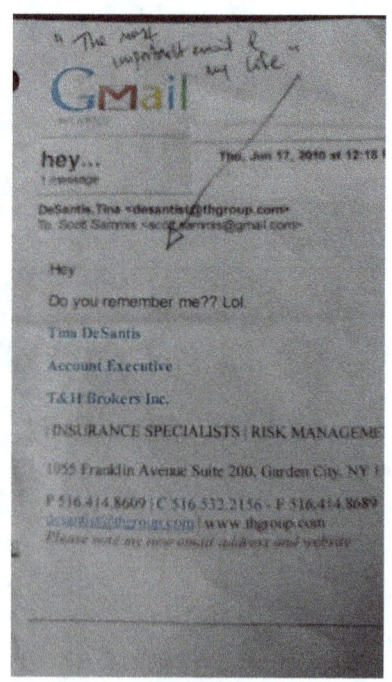

Best email

34

the motorcycle. Holy crap, Batman! We got our shot back! I couldn't get over my euphoria.

The junket across our wide nation was better than I imagined it would be. I tried my best to be in the moment, to enjoy the fabulous national parks, fully experience the long, hard highway miles and the occasionally violent and terrifying weather, but honestly Tina was on my mind the entire time. I emailed her frequently. She had opened a new private gmail account, so we didn't worry about her husband snooping. She seemed genuinely interested in all that happened on the journey, and I detected no jealousy about my travel mate. The days ticked by and I grew more excited to see Tina. On July 20th, I was back!

CHAPTER 7. Breakups

My mom Antoinette died in 1997. Every year since we pick a weekend in the summer to gather her family and my dad's at the Jersey Shore to celebrate her life. It has always been one of my favorite weekends of the year. My mom was an amazing woman, and we felt her presence. One presence we did not feel often was Jim. He religiously elected to refuse to attend the gatherings. I knew he had difficulty socializing in big groups, and my family is rambunctious and fun. To be honest, it upset me in the early years, but I soon came to enjoy not worrying about him interacting with my family.

This Jersey Shore weekend at my favorite cousins Joyce and Michael in Buckhead, NJ, in July 2010, Jim had asked me if he could come, for once. I was shocked and confused. I thought maybe he wanted to work on our marriage. I felt guilty, as I was deep into plans to make my way out of the marriage. I thought maybe he was throwing a Hail Mary pass. I gave him a courtesy "of course," and he came along.

In true Jim fashion, he looked miserable around the family, was unsociable and defiant. He spent most of his time on his cellphone. I wondered why he had asked to come. It would be later when I discovered his girlfriend was unavailable that weekend, and Jim didn't want to be left alone. Lucky me!

He was sulking on the porch of the beautiful Victorian, away from the crowd, and I approached him, requesting he join me on a beach walk. On our walk, I simply said "life is too short to be unhappy all the time. I feel we fight about the most basic matters, and I'm pretty sure you're seeing somebody, so let's either figure it out, or end this. I want to be happy, and with someone who wants the same." He paused a moment, then blurted "I don't like your hair, the way you dress, or your culture." All I could think to say was "OK, then. We can stop this now, and end our 11 year marriage." He didn't respond. I think he really thought I didn't mean it. I had said things like this before. This time I meant if more completely than ever before. The walk back to the house that day in July seemed endless. I was numb. And now I worried how was I going to survive the next day and a half before we drove back to Long Island with by sister and brother-in-law. We were stuck with Jim.

Jim went back to the porch, and I shared the interaction with my family. I was in tears. My dad was furious. "How dare he say those things to my little girl?!" The rest of the family loved and supported me, but they were wary of the eventual outcome. We had fought and made up many times. My family had my back always, and were no big fans of Jim. But they wanted to tread lightly, not sure what was the best thing to do or say for me. "Just in case..."

The ride home up the Jersey shore was awkward beyond

words. I could tell my brother-in-law Dick was biting his tongue. He had a look in his eye like he wanted to tear into Jim to protect me. He didn't, thankfully. I was curiously at peace. I felt relief and certainty. I knew what to do next, and my future felt exciting. The possibilities were endless.

For me the cross country motorcycle venture was the fulfillment of a dream, but also emotionally bittersweet. I knew a breakup was coming with my biker companion. We made it out to California for a wedding in early July, arriving physically and psychologically worn out. A fight occurred over something I thought was trivial, and we didn't speak to each other for several days. Maybe we both knew this trip would be it for us, and were pulling away? The second half of the trip was more business-like; I remember taking a few side trips by myself because she was "too tired." I felt Tina and I had a real chance finally, and that meant saying goodbye to my longtime friend and short time dating partner. I hate goodbyes. Maybe they represent abandonment or loss to me. This one would be bad. As the trip finished up, the third week in July, we were both tired, and tired of each other. We parted, said so long, and spent a few days apart. I was bursting with excitement at my "Hawaii" date with Tina, but in the back of my mind was the dreaded breakup.

CHAPTER 8. The Kiss

Well, it's been a year since our first lunch at 7ᵗʰ Street Cafe, I guess it's time for the next step, dinner. Jim has admitted his affair. I am actively looking for apartments.

I was very excited and nervous about my first dinner with Scott. I wanted to look and feel beautiful. I bought a flirty floral sundress from Lord & Taylor and I needed a private place to get ready for our date. I was still living with Jim and thought it would be bizarre to get ready for a date in front of him, should he happen to be home. Too many awkward questions. So I rented a room at the Marriott so I could be alone to prepare for this important rendezvous.

We decided on a Bayshore seafood restaurant on a Great South Bay - a beautiful location to watch the sunset. I arrived early, ordered a glass of Pino Grigio and waited. My sister Tonianne texted me to see how I was. I told her I was in a beautiful place waiting on friend.

Fat Fish

Our first real date, the day I'd been anticipating for six months, was finally here! What an ocean of water had passed under the bridge. We had false starts, crossed signals, retirements, breakups, reconnections. Leo's in December felt like yesterday, and eons ago, simultaneously. I was late, as usual, stuck on

Tina at Fat Fish

the clotted Sagtikos Parkway. "This is no way to start our honeymoon," I groused to myself, disgusted. I called Tina on her cell to apologize. She was nervous, giddy, giggling. Somehow the word "motel" popped up in the conversation. Whoa, I thought. Did I miss a signal somewhere? We hadn't even kissed yet... I valeted the black Mustang and went to find Tina.

Scott at Fat Fish

Scott walked into the back patio where I was waiting (he was late!) He was wearing a white shirt setting off his tanned skin, blue eyes, and huge smile. I wanted to cry for joy, my heart soared to a place I hadn't recognized or every felt before. I couldn't wait for him to sit next to me and hold me. I had been through so much in the past year. I had no idea my feelings for Scott were this powerful. I was able to free my emotions now that my flawed marriage had finally run its course. I felt a giant release. With Scott now by my side, I had two sips of wine and felt love drunk.

Tina was so gorgeous, radiant, sexy in her perfect little sundress and brilliant smile. This time we hugged for real, no brief business embrace, but a longish, old friend/new lover clutch. What sparks! She already had her wine, I got a rum & coke, and we caught up. So easy, so natural. It felt to me like I'd known and loved Tina my whole life. In reality, it was merely our fifth date.

We moved from the bar to a table on the water. I think the restaurant may have been full, but I didn't notice. My eyes could only see Tina. So much pent up yearning, hoping, wishing. The conversation turned to Tina's favorite niece Stephanie's wedding in New Zealand this coming February. She sadly said she couldn't make the long trip, it was too expensive. She was disappointed. I looked her in the eyes, and said "we're going. No one turns down a chance to experience New Zealand. She's your best buddy as well as your favorite niece. We're going." Tina's mouth fell open, and a huge smile blossomed on her beautiful face. I pressed the case, "would Stephanie cross the Pacific Ocean to go to our wedding?" Of course. "By the way, I imagine a big, joyous wedding with your dad proudly walking his little girl down the aisle, and everybody in tears." I could tell she loved the idea, but she gave me a strange look....

"Do you realize that you have us going to New Zealand, and you have my niece coming across the world to OUR wedding, and you haven't even kissed me yet?

Ok, ok, maybe I do get a little ahead of myself. What I said was "I can fix that." I gave her my best, gentle, lingering, soft "I'll love you forever" kiss. Tina took a deep breath, sunk into her chair, and looked at me...

"Where do I sign the papers?" The kiss helped me let go of one year of pent up emotions. Our chance was here - my ship was finally here. I felt giddy and lightheaded like a teenager - I've never felt so certain of anything in my life. I knew this was the beginning of an amazing love story. I had been waiting to feel this way for 45 years. It blew me away. I did not look back.

Kissing Tina was pure poetry, romance, and dessert. One thing that was unique was the certainty. I felt the tumblers in a complex lock all clicking into place. There would be lots of hurdles, emotional upsets and growth pains, but I had not a single doubt we would surmount them all. Our honeymoon had begun. I could not believe my good fortune.

We managed to actually eat our delicious dinner for the first time. Plans started to be made; trips, apartments, our future together. Although so many obstacles needed to be overcome, I've never felt so certain. The bad part, we had to go our separate homes, me to Jim, and Scott to his Flower Hill home. We left the restaurant giddy, wanting more kisses. Scott had sheepishly asked about the motel: "did I miss something?" I laughed and said "no, the motel was for dressing, not undressing. I'm not that kind of girl." He seemed relieved. The valet brought his hot black Mustang around to pick us up. As I got in I noticed how handsome he looked behind the wheel.

Neither one of us wanted this night to end. He pulled up next to where my VW Jetta was parked, and I invited him into my car - I figured the stick shift in his car would be problematic. We got into the Jetta and the sparks started flying, kissing, groping, and then it happened - my tears started to pour out of my eyes uncontrollably. It had been 15 years since my lips touched another man's, and I was totally unprepared how to react. I felt relief, guilt, euphoria - and sadness. This meant a true and definite end to my tortured marriage to Jim. There were no doubts. I finally found my true soul mate, the love of my life.

CHAPTER 9. Loose Ends

We talked, texted and emailed everyday, often multiple times. My August was very booked. All I wanted to do was spend every minute with Tina, but two big commitments got in the way. Our annual Sammis family reunion with my sisters, their husbands and seven nephews and nieces took up two weeks on Fire Island, and I had arranged months ago to take my three kids to Alaska. One week was on the 10 passenger cruise ship The Pacific Catalyst, and another week in the Denali National Park. I remember walking at night on Fire Island singing to Tina's voicemail. "I just want to say I love you, I just want to say I really care," and other oldies but goodies made it into the queue. I missed her terribly, but knew we had to be patient. So far I hadn't pushed too hard or too fast, and we finally had our chance. We met on a few chance occasions between Fire Island and Alaska, including one more passionate make out session after a Fat Fish dinner and a few lunches. We both couldn't wait for late August to get our 40 year honeymoon started. Finally.

Most of my August was spent looking for apartments, working hard at the office (I was determined not to let this all effect my work), and dreaming of my new future. Jim was still in denial that I was really going to leave. I saw Scott as much as we possibly could. It may sound strange, but I wanted to be in my own apartment before I fully committed to a new relationship. I was looking forward to my new independence and freedom. Scott was busy traveling with his children. They were about to embark on their first adventure since they lost their beloved wife and mother, and I was thrilled for them. I hadn't met the kids, but imagined they were wonderful human beings.

Labor Day was approaching and Jim asked me if I wanted to take a motorcycle ride to New York City. We were breaking up the way we had to - gently. After our ride we came home, opened a bottle of bubbly, and toasted to us, and to our new beginnings - very bizarre. I got a little drunk and told him how I met someone I was crazy about. I told him all about Scott, and begged him to confess his affair. He cried and left to meet her. I was drunk and excited. Scott was in Alaska with his kids. I called to tell him of the new revelation, and how there were no more secrets. His reaction was a little nervous. He had no idea what was in store. This was moving fast!

I watched my cellphone like a hawk as we cruised Alaska's Inner Passage, hoping for any kind of call coverage. I needed to hear Tina's voice. I only got one or two fleeting chances. When the cruise was complete, the kids and I found our way to the Petersburg, AK airport and boarded a local jet for Fairbanks. It would make several stops along the way.

On one of those stops, after some passengers got off and

some new ones embarked, my cell phone surprised me by chirping in my pocket. It was Tina! And it was 7:30pm Alaska time, so it had to be 11:30 pm Eastern Tina Time. Elated, I excused myself from a conversation to take the call in the back of the plane. Tina was giddy. "I told Jim about you! It's all out! No more secrets. I feel so free!" Holy crap, Batman. I had visions of jealous Jim hunting me down. But at the same time I was ecstatic. We were taking risks, rolling forward in a hurry. Wow. This was going to be some ride!

CHAPTER 10. Forging Ahead

Scott came back from Alaska, and we made plans to meet as soon as he landed. We could not wait. We were like school kids at Christmas. We met at Milk & Sugar in Bayshore for coffee and a walk to the ferry. We didn't have time for much more. Scott wondered, with a twinkle in his eye, if I had rented another hotel room to get ready. I know you're ready, I smiled, but not yet. Soon.

We ended up leaning up against the side of my car in a passionate kiss. I wasn't used to PDAs in places like ferry parking lots, and was uncomfortable. A woman passing by in

Milk & Sugar

a car, hunting for a spot, shouted "Looks like fun!" The topic turned to the elephant in the room. When are we going to consummate this new relationship??? I left it in Scott's hands....

Was I a tad bit anxious to get this important element of our romance going? Hell, yes. It had been 13 months since I had declared my undying love at the 7th Street Cafe. So I got a room at the Courtyard @ Marriot in Farmingdale, didn't tell her, but asked her to meet me at Houlihan's Restaurant, right next door, for a drink. She showed up on time, looking drop dead gorgeous, but not sure what was on the agenda. After our drink I suggested we move the party to the bar at the nearby Courtyard. She gave me a sideways glance, and said "Let's go." I was still reluctant to push too hard or fast, for fear of blowing it.

Houlihan's

The Yankees were on the tube at the second bar, so we sipped another drink and waited, for what? Excruciating silence. Tina seemed almost to be enjoying watching me marinate. After too long I said "I have a room upstairs. If you like we can just watch TV." She smiled coquettishly and nodded. Up we went. I brought her a "Principessa" t shirt and some other little gifts. They must have melted her heart. The anticipation was killing us, the TV never went on, but once we started, it was a magnificent conflagration. When we came up for air, it was well past midnight.

If we didn't have obligations, it's possible we'd still be there. Tina had to return to the apartment. As she drove away, there were tears streaming down her face.

The next time Scott and I were able to get together was Labor Day evening. I didn't feel comfortable dating frequently with Jim still in my apartment. We agreed to meet at a restaurant called Cafe Toscano. There was a hurricane in the forecast, which might make things interesting. We found our table, totally love drunk and unable to hide the sheer joy of being together. For some reason, both Jim and I were still wearing our wedding rings. I had a move out date of September 18th, but I was still there until then. Scott and I like to hold hands everywhere, but this is difficult as I have an Italian habit of speaking with my hands. I was nervously playing with my ring while trying to make a point when - OOPS - the wedding ring popped off my finger and flipped, slow motion, across the open space to our left, and disappeared.

I thought to myself as the ring sailed off her finger "this is a wonderful omen. The gods are smiling on us." I remember she told the waiter "oh, it's no big deal, forget about it. Maybe you'll find it later." I shook my head, to myself, and redoubled my efforts.

I didn't care about the ring. I said "leave it." Scott and the waiter frantically searched everywhere for it, and eventually found it. I no longer had an attachment to it.

Wearing it had become just habit.

Scott suggested he show me his home in Huntington. I'd never seen it before. He wanted me to see the home he hoped we'd someday share. We braved the "hurricane" which never really materialized. The "weather guessers" blew it again. I couldn't wait, but I'd told him I also couldn't make love for a few days. Our first four hour marathon left me with an uncomfortable UTI. After some weeks of dormancy, the Courtyard experience had thrown my system for a loop.

We arrived at Scott's home - a beautiful center hall colonial with a barking dog, and full of life and too many things. He asked me if I could envision myself living here? Absolutely. When we toured his bedroom, I couldn't help myself. I begged him to make love to me. To hell with the UTI. He awoke passion in me that I thought had died long ago. Although he was severely tempted, he thought better of it, for the long run, and held me off.

28 Flower Hill Road

50

I've always hated goodbyes, even sometimes deciding not to start a potentially decent relationship just to avoid the goodbye at the end. Ending my relationship with my friend and motorcycle partner kept me up at night. I'd known her for many years before her divorce and our subsequent dating, and I respected the journey of her life. I knew this breakup would hurt her, so I gathered input from a few trusted friends on how to do it gracefully and firmly. The best way was in person at a frequently visited place. We both arrived separately on our Harleys, as she was expecting a further ride together. She was always up for a ride. I said we needed to talk for a minute, so we took a walk. Since my dinner with Tina at Fat Fish in July, a distinct chill, accompanied by distance, had settled into our relationship. I had spent most of August away, and she had taken another long bike adventure with a different group. I screwed up my courage and said "We both know something is missing in this relationship, and we've lost a lot since the trip. If we were going strong, I never would have been attracted to someone else. But I have been, and I want to pursue it." Ever the proud and defiant one, she cut me off, giving me the new rules: "Don't ever call me. EVER." She walked back to her bike and left. I felt horrible, but I knew she was a strong survivor, and would be OK. For my part, what I felt was enormous relief. Onward!

CHAPTER 11. 83 Wisconsin Street

Long Beach is one of my favorite places. It's been a dream of mine to live between the sea and the bay, with a magical two mile boardwalk meant to cleanse the soul. My landlords' names were Antoinette and Nick, identical to my parents. I felt the Antoinette LaMagra (my mom) intervention here again. The home was fully furnished in a tacky seashore motif. I felt it was a perfect place for me to escape and rebuild. I felt the winter months in Long Beach would be quite ideal for my journey.

Tina called all excited. She'd found a winter rental in Long Beach and wanted me to come check it out. I was to meet her at a cafe on the main drag. She got there first...

It was a beautiful, sunny, warm September afternoon when I signed my lease. I asked Scott to meet me at the local restaurant Beech Street Cafe to hopefully show him my new nest. I arrived first to the pub (Scott had an hour commute from Huntington to Long Beach), ordered a glass

Beech Street Cafe

of white wine, and waited for my prince. He walked through the tavern doors just as the song "I can see clearly now, the rain is gone" was playing on the sound system over my head. Again I felt a sign from Antoinette. He took my breath away.

When I was a preteen I developed a major, full blown crush on Scott Baio, my sisters can attest. In any event, the huge flutter my heart felt when Scott Baio came on the TV came to my mind. I eventually came out of my crush, and never fully felt that same flutter until that day watching my Scott Sammis walk through the restaurant doors with his confidence and his smile. We were officially a couple. 83 Wisconsin Street, Long Beach would be our starting place, and I never felt happiness like this. I didn't know it existed.

I helped Tina move her belongings into 83 Wisconsin Street, Long Beach on September 18th, her first day. Half my blood, my genetics, are from Wisconsin – my mom was born in Monroe, Wisconsin, the "Swiss Cheese Capital of the United States" - so I naturally felt the street name was a good luck talisman. The apartment was compact, beachy

Tina at 83 Wisconsin St

and welcoming. We felt instantly at home. No sooner did her clothes fill up the drawers than we were exploring all the horizontal surfaces. I never felt so alive. We could not get enough of each other.

That first Saturday was more of the same. We took a break to visit a nearby Kohl's for some house supplies. The parking lot was packed. We entered the store in a fog of infatuation. When we'd collected our stuff, we attempted to find the car. Impossible. So love blind were we that the car simply disappeared. Poof. Gone. 2000 pounds of metal and glass had evaporated. Ten minutes into a frantic search - I mean we had NO idea even what area it was in - we finally got close enough for the clicker fob to communicate with the Jetta. Jeez.

I've always understood that women tend to lose their sex drive in their mid 40s, and I had been experiencing just that. I accepted the seemingly unavoidable truth. So many of my friends were going through it. I didn't feel like an outsider with that emotion. Well, was I mistaken. My lovemaking with Scott was explosive, mind shattering, simply euphoric. Our connections were urgent. We could not get enough of each other. It started to get embarrassing. Wait staff in restaurants would frequently comment to us "you two look so in love." We were love inebriated. Jackie Collins romance novels had nothing on us!

There wasn't a single thing we could do about this tidal wave of passion. If they were paying attention, people in parking spaces near the Long Beach boardwalk could have caught us repeatedly *inflagrante* in our cars. I believe one van load of Baptists may actually have witnessed the craziness. I know one cop rapped on our back seat window when the entire car was fogged up in a Babylon church parking lot late one night. What could we do? It was imperative. Nuts.

My sister Tonianne is an extremely important person in my life. She is the oldest of five children, and I am the youngest. We are 11 years apart, and she was instrumental in my upbringing. She has always been my closest confidante. She was consumed with curiosity about my new love. On the first Friday after moving in she strongly suggested she come over for dinner and to meet Scott. Tonianne and the rest of my beloved family have only wanted my happiness. They witnessed years of unhappiness, turmoil, and quite frankly a bit of mental abuse in my relationship with Jim. I told Tonianne quite a bit about Scott, how patient, kind, brilliant and loving he is. I told her of his tragedy. She needed to witness this herself, and give the stamp of approval to the others.

Tonianne arrived that first Friday after we moved in to 83 Wisconsin Street with our "beautiful cousin" Rose, who we love and care for, especially since both her parents are gone. Scott greeted them with his tender and welcoming smile and big open armed hug (signature of his). And that's all they needed. They were sold. Dinner was flawless, comfortable and reassuring. Tonianne's smile was bright and telling. She felt her sister was in the hands of a man who would lift her up, and relish the closeness of their big, happy Italian family. Tonianne gave her stamp of approval to the rest of the family. And so, the whirlwind of phone calls began.

September 23rd, it was time for one of the most critical introductions of my lifetime. I brought Tina to 28 Flower Hill Road to meet the other three most important people in my life: Trevor, Becky and John. They, of course, had heard me gushing about her for many months. They well remembered the intervention in the spring to make sure I didn't settle, and that I continue to reach for my dreams, and pursue Tina. In a real way, they could claim ownership of our relationship.

When Tina and I came into the kitchen Becky and John were in the middle of making pesto sauce for a pasta dinner. They had fallen in love with pesto sauce in Cinque Terre, Italy when

Kitchen in a happy time

they visited shortly after their mom died, and it was an emotional favorite. They turned to us and gave Tina a 1000 watt smile. They seemed genuinely delighted. My heart soared. You worry about these things, but I shouldn't have been surprised. I'd told them nearly every detail of our courtship so far. Nearly.

The kids were in a fairly sustainable place, nearly five years after the tragedy. Becky and Trevor had stable relationships, John was in between. He had decided to pursue his medical degree, and was 100% involved in the effort. They welcomed Tina with open arms, and I felt a part of our promise coming true. In the immediate nightmare of losing Mary, the remaining four of us each swore to reach out, selectively, and bring a fantastic mate to the group, one for each us, to eventually total eight. I felt proud to have fulfilled the promise, shown that it could be done, and lead by example. Tina was my choice of soul mate, and a proud addition to our family.

Scott arranged a night for me to meet his three children, Becky, Trevor and John. I was nervous, but from how Scott described them, and knowing him, I knew they would be amazing people. Ironically it was Jim's birthday.

I walked into 28 Flower Hill, and was greeted by their barking dog Niko, and Becky and John. Wow, beautiful smiles and warm hugs. I immediately fell in love with them. They had special beer, they walked me into the garden to pick tomatoes for the salad. I felt my future with them would be full of love.

CHAPTER 12. October Acceleration

We both knew. 100% Certain. Beyond a shadow of a doubt. Storm clouds be damned. In the first week of October, we trekked up to the magical town of Woodstock, NY to the Wild Rose Inn, a ridiculously romantic Victorian hotel. We did manage to escape the room a few times, one of which was to have dinner at Joshua's, where I proposed. Mind you, this was not entirely appropriate. It was barely nine weeks after our Fat Fish first date. And she was married. No matter. Stars were in our eyes. The future pulled us like a giant magnet. Nothing could stand in our way....

Wild Rose Inn

It's October. We spent a delirious two weeks in Long Beach. Scott and I are moving full speed ahead. We're certain, we're madly in love, and we're planning our future. In the meantime Jim and I had a pretty courteous separation, which left many perplexed. We had a friendship, or so I thought, that could withstand a separation. We spoke about how silly it is to never speak again to a person you once shared a life with. We thought we had a unique and gentle way to stay in good standing with each other. Little did I know, Jim had a plan. Little did he know, I was already far gone.

Jim and I agreed that we would get together occasionally on a Sunday to watch our favorite team, the Dallas Cowboys...

"This is a Bad Idea," I thought when Tina proposed seeing Jim for Dallas games on Sundays. I have severe reservations. My fear always was Jim would pull out all the emotional stops at some point this fall, she would weaken, soft heart that she is, and they would fall back into bed. I put those fears aside, banished to a compartment in the back of my head, and honored Tina's instincts.

The first - and last- time Jim and I put this Cowboy plan into action, I quickly felt uncomfortable. I had just come off one of the most romantic weekends imaginable with Scott in Woodstock at the Wild Rose Inn where he proposed marriage, and there had been no hesitation in my answer. Nothing in my life had ever felt so right. Slight wrinkle: I hadn't asked for a divorce yet.

So the game is on the TV, Jim made my favorite pasta dish, and opened a bottle of my favorite wine. We watched the first half, just like old times. But I couldn't help wondering, is this an attempt at a reconciliation? I thought it was understood, we were going to be friends. Now I'm confused about his intentions, but not about mine. Jim started to make moves that reminded me of our first date. I started to feel very uncomfortable. Half time came, and I knew I had to go. I gave the excuse of being tired. At the door, he went in for a lip kiss, but I only offered my cheek and a warm hug. I drove back to Long Beach glad to be out of the awkward situation, feeling like I dodged a bullet. I thought it best not to return for another game.

Part of the bizarre, courteous separation dance Tina and Jim were engaged in included the gradual, piecemeal migration of her belongings from their former apartment to 83 Wisconsin Street. After three or four partial pick ups I said "enough." "Tina, make arrangements to collect ALL of your stuff. I will bring my big red Ram 1500 pickup, and we'll get it done." OK she said, hesitantly.

We arrived one October weekend afternoon at the apartment. Jim had staged a fair amount of Tina's collection in boxes on the kitchen table, ready to go. He was surprising cordial, immediately offering me a beer and Tina some wine.

I certainly didn't envision this visit as an extended social call, so I looked at Tina for a second. She accepted, and so did I. I began to haul the stack of boxes off the table out to the truck. They chatted, and browsed a box of photographs. About 20 minutes into our happy little vignette, I started to squirm, internally. I knew Tina had a hope chest her mom had left her that she wanted. I suggested we grab it, just to move the party along, you know? Jim agreed, and up the stairs we filed to their loft bedroom. He went up first, Tina next, and I brought up the rear. There on the night stand were a mostly empty bottle of Scotch, and a sawed off shotgun. "Hmmm," I thought, "that's fascinating," as my mind instantly conjured up an image of me hurtling backwards out the second story window with a gaping shotgun wound in my chest.

"Jeeyum!" Tina scolded, "what's this about?" He paused a second and said "I've been a little depressed lately (I gulped) and the Scotch helps me to sleep." It seemed to me like he may have practiced these answers. "This isn't the nicest neighborhood, and Jodi (his girlfriend) sometimes visits late at night, so I have this (shotgun) for security." I assumed it might have something to do with showing me who was boss in this situation. I cleared my throat, and offered "How about that hope chest?" Refocused, we hauled it out to the truck. I shook Jim's hand, thanked him for the beer (not the show), and got in the truck. They exchanged a few words, and Tina joined me. Yikes.

My separation from Jim confused and confounded many. Where some people expected anger and emotional fireworks, there was gentleness, friendship, and what I thought would be a kind and mature parting. By mid October I needed to take the next step, to ask for the divorce. It would be easy, right? Boy, was I ever wrong about that.

The warning signs of Jim's reality were there. The first call came the first day I was officially out of our apartment and into my new Long Beach nest. Did Jim not see me moving my things out for two weeks prior? It hit him that first September day, when he came home and the house was mostly empty of my things. His first call to me was the hardest. His tears were flowing and frantic, and he pleaded to me that this was a big mistake.

After the sadness, came the anger, followed by the threats of suicide. As disturbing and sad as it was, all the outbursts made my decision much clearer. My time -13 years- worrying about Jim's emotional state was finally done.

Soon I mustered up the courage to ask for the divorce. Jim's response to the request was "I thought I'd go my way for a bit, you'd go your way, and we'd find our way back to each other." I did not lead him on to believe that things would work out this time. It was true, in the past, numerous times, we would fight bitterly, forgive, and carry on. This time was different. I was physically and mentally out the door. I had a destination.

My sister Nancy and niece Stephanie, my two other soul mates, were in town for Stephanie's bridal shower which was held on Halloween weekend. Scott was in Key West, FL writing a memoir to his lost beloved wife Mary Lou. He needed to close that chapter of his life, and he was ready. His favorite author is Earnest Hemingway, and Key West was the perfect place to honor his memories of Mary Lou. I was thrilled for him, and could not wait to read his rough draft. While Scott was away he sent me three dozen roses, and paid for a dinner for me and all the ladies. He had already won the hearts of these ladies, and they hadn't physically met him yet. My happiness was obvious and infectious, and that's all they needed to see.

My niece Stephanie and I share many of the same personal traits. She is someone who views the world similarly to me. She had made some colorful relationship choices in the past, as had I, but possessed a bit more confidence than me to get out, mostly unscathed. When Stephanie brought Steve into our lives we all knew he was "the one." His kind and beautiful smile, his confidence and good looks, and his adoring glances at our Stephanie sold us all. Many times I said to myself, "I want that. I want someone to love and be loved by in that way." This man, Steve Muir, and his love for my niece, set the bar for my expectations. I tell them that from time to time. Stephanie and Steve are *part of the reason I was able to imagine a different relationship, break away, and find my true happiness.*

On my bucket list for years was to write a book about my marriage and the tragedy of Mary's death. Six months after her passing I began a life-changing psychological session with my counselor Dee. It was Dee, in the early going, who got me to realize my biggest fear, in this loss, was that I would crawl into an emotional fetal state, and never have another warm, fulfilling relationship. If I didn't do the work necessary to fully grieve, internalize and process the body blow of her death, I would be stuck forever in a numbed, fearful never never land. I wanted to love again. And it was Dee, at the end of the book writing, when I was struggling with how to complete the final chapter, who helped me realize the purpose, and the title, of the book: to say "Goodbye, Mary Lou." I had been a journal writer since a crisis in mid-marriage, and had chronicled the fateful Africa vacation in some detail. I carried a bundle of emotions from the marriage and the tragedy with me everyday. I felt the need to express, to push out all of that, and store it safely in printed form. I couldn't keep going over it endlessly. I hated leaving Tina's side, but she would be busy with a family wedding shower, and I eagerly anticipated writing all day in my favorite place.

So I hauled the 12 years of journals down to a perfect water view room at The Reef Hotel on the north side of Key

West Island. The island has the gentle breezes, Bahamian and pirate influences, and the subtle feeling that this is as far in the continental US that one can run to (as Hemingway did) that made it perfect for me to create. After an intense effort to organize this big life of ours and to come to grips with the tragedy, the writing started to flow. It was cathartic. The week passed in a blur of tears, revelations and warm satisfaction. My brain and heart could take a break from carrying around all these emotions and contradictions. They, and the story, were captured on paper once and for all. The result was <u>Goodbye, May Lou</u>. I felt lighter as I boarded the AA flight back to JFK and my new life with Tina.

CHAPTER 13. Diamonds, Stars and Bakery Faces

November in Long Beach was magical - the end of fall. The days were clear and crisp, and the nights were getting longer and colder, which meant the crowds were gone. Scott and I walked the boardwalk hand in hand every chance we could get, planning our future while we looked out to the sea. Scott had asked me to marry him in October, but we did not yet purchase a ring. One evening we were dining in an elegant new restaurant in the Alegria Hotel on the boardwalk. We were love drunk and couldn't wait to get back to 83 Wisconsin to fall back into bed. On our walk back, continuously stopping for another kiss and hug, Scott asked if we could pick out a ring and order it on the website Blue Nile, a well respected jewelry wholesaler where you can design your own ring without hassle. I was thrilled but a little nervous as well. No one knew we had decided to get married.

We were giddy looking over the vast selection of rings and settings in all shapes and sizes. There was a mouse controlled sliding scale regarding the diamond size/cost. I jokingly pushed the slider to 13 carats on one ring - $10 million! Scott's eyebrows raised. We moved the mouse back *into the real world and Scott ordered the most beautiful halo diamond ring a girl could dream of. We were official!!!*

The first travel adventure of our 40 year honeymoon started in Wenham, MA at our annual thanksgiving family reunion, hosted by my sister Sue, husband Tom, and daughters Emily and Meg. The ring had been delivered but we left it home - not ready for the public just yet. Our three children always joined us. We cooked together, laughed and invariably tried some new activity: candle pin bowling, fencing and costume shopping had been on the agenda in past years. This year's BIG NEWS was Tina. Everyone had heard all about her from me, and the Massachusetts family embraced her enthusiastically. Well, that was up until she kicked our asses in this years' activity: regular bowling. My sister Sue accused me of "bringing in a ringer," and to get back at Tina (me) she hid the blow up moose head that was the coveted winner's prize. In spite of the accusations of cheating and the demands for a recount, Tina reveled in the warmth of the family, and felt completely accepted.

We arose at 4:00am the Friday after Thanksgiving to catch an early flight to Arizona, the destination a favorite dude ranch of Tina's called Stage Coach Trails Ranch . She LOVES horses, would be happy mucking out stables, wrangling horses and managing tack all so she could be near them. Tina is a good, competent rider, me not so much. Our first day Tina was out with one other advanced rider and

Craig the wrangler, running, cantering and loping. I went out with the eight year olds on the glue horses and sweated my ass off. That night at dinner, the female proprietor of the ranch approached us and opined that I was a good enough rider to go on a serious run tomorrow. I almost felt flattered.

Tina had fallen in love with her horse of the previous day, Stetson, and was reunited for our second day. When Craig asked Tina how it was riding Stetson, she said "like butta." I didn't get yesterday's mount, Elmer, but instead was paired with a horse named Lightning or Nitroglycerin or Rocket, I forget which. Having had my lower internal organs reorganized and mashed previously on horseback, I was prepared this time for the pounding: three pairs of tidy whitey underwear, bicycle shorts and blue jeans.

We took off walking at first, soon arriving at a sandy creek bed where Craig stopped and turned around to ask "Are you ready?" Tina sang out in the affirmative, I croaked out a tepid OK. Bam, like a shot, we were off, on a dead run. Tina was nervous. I was panic stricken. I had been instructed how to use my legs to work with the horse to minimize the jarring, but my butt and nearby private parts were slamming up and DOWN in the saddle. Three thoughts rushed into my head::(1)"I'm going to kill her, (2) How will I do it? Sword, knife, poison?; (3) I think I just soiled myself!" Just before I passed out, Craig pulled up, turned and asked "You OK back there?" I just whimpered. Tina, I noticed, was wracked with gut-wrenching guffaws. Perfect.

I was so nervous for Scott, riding at that breakneck pace. I have a terrible habit of hysterical laughter when I'm nervous. Not sure my bouts of hysteria were appreciated at that moment. I couldn't help it. It WAS funny.

Not wanting to die out here in the desert, I agreed to carry on. After a few more runs, I got a little more familiar with the hell bent running. Or maybe the combination of endorphins and adrenalin just anesthetized me. Anyway, we packed up, I took some Tylenol, and we left for the Grand Canyon the next morning. My back was surprisingly OK. The onions, not so much.

I loved the dude ranch. If my mother were alive, she could attest she made the mistake of agreeing to my repeated request "When I'm eight years old, you'll buy me a horse, right?" Well, 8 turned into 45 and I still craved owning a horse. I had found this dude ranch 10 years earlier, on a search to indulge my horse ownership fantasy. The dude ranches in NY are meant for everything but horseback riding. Out in Needles, Arizona it was about me, the horse, and the land. Authentic Western riding, no holds barred., no TVs, no phone. We were out in the Wild West, and I loved every minute of it. Scott may not have shared my enthusiasm as thoroughly as I did, but he never let on! I figured it was New Love.

I'd never been to the Grand Canyon, so the second part of our journey was to visit the famous national park and then head to Las Vegas for a day or two in Sin City. The weather was unusually cold and snowy. We had to get long johns at Walmart. The views were awe inspiring, the colors and contrasts were out of a story book. I wanted to hike and stay right in the canyon, except we would have died from exposure. We stayed at an adorable mountain resort which was pretty desolate this time of year.

I had been struggling with the whole marriage and honesty thing. The revelation that Jim had been cheating for over a year really rocked me. At the same time at work, a young man I'd known for years, newly married himself, had come on to me. After a drink or two at dinner, my anger and sense of betrayal took hold of me, and raised its ugly head to challenge my new love and freedom.

At the Salcon Restaurant in our resort our first night in Grand Canyon, we had a few drinks, and Tina brought up an unusual topic. A young man at work, Dylan, kept making unwanted passes at her. She mentioned he was recently married, and she seemed quite annoyed. To me, Tina was the most dazzling, desirable woman in the world, so I knew I would have to cope with a number of suitors, especially now since she was "on the market." I wondered why she would bring him up, on this, the inaugural trip of our 40 year honeymoon. I heard echoes of times Mary would make me jealous at parties or dinners. The same nasty feeling rose up in my gut, and I felt myself quieting and withdrawing from the conversation. This was my go to response: "just go silent until the moment blows over."

From years of counseling and introspection, I knew how resentment poisoned most marriages, including my own to Mary. Each time we felt scared, instead of opening up and admitting our vulnerability, we went all John Wayne, tough and independent. "I don't care! I don't want to get into it! It'll blow over, and mean nothing in a day or two." WRONG. Each time that happens, another invisible brick is set in a wall of resentment between the couple. After enough episodes, the wall is so high, it can't be breached, and the marriage is unrecoverable. You've seen these couples, sleepwalking through their marriages, not talking, staring at their cell phones at dinner. I was bound and determined NOT to let resentment take the honeymoon away from Tina and me.

Back at the hotel room after dinner there was that too familiar silence/distance, and I couldn't let a brick, even one, get set between us. It was uncomfortable for me to tell my John Wayne to sit down and shut up. "Tina," I said, "I'm worried, and I feel a little scared. I don't want to lose you, and I hate it when you're mad at me. Mentioning Dylan at dinner made me feel there are so many guys, some younger and better than me, that want you. I feel a little vulnerable."

Scott opened up to me up in the hotel room after dinner.

71

He said he felt vulnerable. My heart went out to him. It made me realize how Jim's affair affected me. If Dylan was a would be cheater like Jim, why wouldn't all men be the same? Why would Scott be different? For a brief moment at dinner I felt I couldn't trust any man, and I was scared. I had been hurt badly, and did not deal with it. Scott and I cried and talked and talked. We made a promise to each other to talk every issue out, not take the easy way out and put it off. We decided that our relationship would be a NO BRICK ZONE. Then it was on to Vegas!

One idea I offered to explain why everyone feels threatened and scared occasionally, can act defensively, and say things that wind up being invisible bricks, is the amygdala, our "reptile brain." Different parts of our brains are busy with managing the magnificent machines we live it, other parts with planning and decision making. The amygdala has been handed down to us to protect us, to be on constant alert to threats. Reptiles have highly developed amygdalas to help them manage a hostile environment. Our inner little children serve a similar protective purpose. They say "Watch out! We've been hurt before, and this situation seems EXACTLY like when we got hurt!" Well, in truth, the situations in adulthood are rarely as threatening as they seem to our reptile brain protectors. It can help in these times to realize this, calm down, and realize we aren't in much danger. Tina and I found a couple of tools to help us from brick laying. I thought we had a diamond crusted method of keeping our love affair from dying of slowly building resentment. How exciting!

We finished off our little post Thanksgiving adventure with a night at the Paris Hotel in Las Vegas. My back felt somewhat tight after the long drive from the canyon to Vegas. I was amazed it was behaving so well in the aftermath of the galloping riverbed experience. The solicitous check in clerk offered "Mr. Sammis, for an extra $50 we can upgrade you to a suite, how does that sound?" I felt like a big shot, and accepted. The suite was enormous. In it was a massive bathroom with an appliance Tina had never encountered. "What's that?" "It's a bidet. Here, let me show you how it works." I bent over at the waist, found the water faucet and turned it. Water shot straight into my face. Surprised, I jerked upright and WHAM, out went my back. Unfortunate welcome to Vegas, but the painkillers quickly kicked in, and we were off to explore.

In front of the Bakery Face patisserie

I'd been to Vegas before, and on my brief visit, I was not favorably impressed. This time it seemed to make sense that we end our little vacation there as we had to fly out of McCarran Airport. Scott had booked us at the Paris Hotel. Fancy! I was really excited to stay in such a luxury hotel. The shops were elegant, the restaurants exquisite, and the French bakery.....We walked to the Patisserie in the Paris Hotel to get a cup of coffee. Entering the bakery, smelling the heavenly aromas, it hit me that this sensation was what my heart felt every time I looked at my new man. We both recognized the look on each other's face: deep contentment, anticipation, pleasure, just "ahhhhh." At the same time we both said "bakery face." Scott was was my new home. He made me feel pure joy, comfort.

CHAPTER 14. Christmas on Two Coasts

December is here, two years after we first met in the lobby of 125 Froehlich Farm Blvd., and a year since we made plans in Leo's Pub for a dinner/drinks in the New Year. They turned out to be false hope, and a false start. But, what a difference a year makes! We did not get off the ground last December, but now we're absolutely soaring.

Early in the month we took a weekend ride out to the North Fork wineries with Scott's oldest friend Fred and his lovely second chance wife Pat. We fell in love with the Tuscany themed winery Raphael.

Raphael Winery

The red roof tiles, the ornate chandeliers, the dark wood, the intimacy of the place, it was all magical in my eyes. We were so swept away that we inquired about wedding dates for 2011. They had no Saturdays or Sundays left, only Fridays. Hell bent, love drunk, bakery faced, we booked Friday September 9th. We may have overlooked a few details: (1) we hadn't announced our engagement; (2) working people we wanted at the wedding would undoubtedly have a difficult time attending on a Friday; and (3) I wasn't certain I'd even be divorced by then. Oh, what the hell? Damn the torpedoes, full speed ahead! An intervention was necessary.

In hindsight, we may have been acting a little hastily. We were certainly ready for wedding bells, but was everybody else? In late November, I had asked Tina's father Nick for her hand on the telephone. He hadn't met me yet – that would come at New Years when I planned to come to Florida – but Nick had heard enough from the family grapevine – the sisters vetting committee – that he happily gave his permission. More people in Florida knew than in New York.

The cat scrambled out of the bag in December when Tina was visiting the family in Florida. She showed the new engagement

Beautiful Ring

76

ring to her family, and Facebook maven Michele posted one picture. The news spread like wildfire, except to non-Facebookers like me.

While Tina was in Florida enjoying sharing her big news story, I was in California with the three kids on our annual Christmas pilgrimage. My favorite parts of the gathering are the communal meals, the everyday mass walks, and the hilarious white elephant gift exchange. We parted and drove down from Gold Country to the SF peninsula to stay with Aunt Sally overnight, before our early morning flight to NY. At dinner with Emily, the kids' cousin, she was ebullient, but my kids were subdued. I got the feeling I was missing something, out of the loop. Emily was bursting, while at the same time the kids wouldn't look me in the eye. Very unusual. Finally Cousin Em couldn't take it any longer and blurted "I'm SO happy you're getting married! I saw the ring on Facebook." I was dumbfounded, sheepish. My plan was to break the news to the kids at some near future date, not this way. "Dad, it's so SOON." "Why didn't you tell us?" "Isn't Tina still married to Jim?" I got defensive. I felt like I'd committed some horrible, unforgivable atrocity. My lowest point is when I feel like I've let down someone I love. What an awful feeling, looking at the disappointed, concerned faces of my most important loved ones. We'd been through hell together, and stayed shoulder to shoulder, arm in arm. We were "the four of us," we'd made promises. Was I really going to make it "the five of us" without consulting them?

In truth, since Mary died, we hadn't been as honest with each other as we could have. For one thing, when I finally started haltingly dipping my toe in the dating pool, I went to great pains to keep my dates secret. When one eventually seemed a little promising, I mentioned it to them. The boys seemed OK, but Becky said "Keep it to yourself. I don't want to know a single thing about any of your dating, until you have someone you're going to marry." I did my best to honor that request. Becky had also reacted vehemently to a nascent plan I had to ride across the country with a motorcycle group in 2008. "Dad, we already lost mom, I'm not taking a chance on losing you too!," she sobbed. OK, no trip. Maybe I was overly sensitive about anything that would mean "taking me away from them" or replacing their mom?

I assured them as best I could, and apologized for not telling them, but then I began to feel some anger welling up. Were they trying to deny me happiness? Other families would have screamed and cried and hashed out the differences. Not us. In a tradition passed down from both of my parents, and practiced by Mary's family also, we tended to go to our corners, pout, lick our wounds, and convince ourselves "it'll pass." Not good, too many bricks. It looked like we were going to board the plane the next day in a bad place. There would be many emotional miles to negotiate, more tears, and bad feelings. For the first time, I felt storm clouds on the horizon.

After Mary passed, Scott and his kids started a tradition of spending Christmas in California with Mary's family. Mary's sister Amy has a huge farmhouse in Amador County, up in the gold country of Northern California., which hosted the big crowd for the holidays. It was good for their souls. Scott admitted later that he often felt lonely out there, mostly missing Mary. We thought it strange to be spending the holidays apart, but things were happening so fast.

I had booked a flight to Florida to be with my dad and the rest of the gang. Scott and I would be together on New Years, back in Florida, so my family could meet my true love. My family knew of the engagement, as Scott had asked my dad for his permission in November. No one else knew, most importantly, Scott's kids.

This was all very foreign to me – my heart being on fire for Scott. I thought I was through the heartache from my marriage to Jim ending and my sadness for his grasping. Jim and I had so many problems, but the holidays were a special time for us.

At the airport on Christmas Eve, with a flight to Florida seriously delayed, my cell phone rang. It was Jim. We both cried hysterically at the sound of each others' voices. So many emotions. Jim was pleading that we shouldn't end, and this was all a mistake. I knew for me it was not a mistake, but I was wracked with sadness at the death of our dream, and that Jim was hurting so badly.

The holidays in Florida were exactly what I needed, loving family, exuberance about my engagement to Scott, and a sign of relief from them that my difficult time with Jim was through. They felt they had me back again. Loads of pictures were taken, one in particular showed clearly my beautiful shiny new engagement. ring - Bam- right on Facebook. My nephew's girlfriend Michele was a Facebook junkie. No one was safe.

It turns out there were real storms to contend with, in addition to the emotional ones. At the San Francisco airport we learned the East Coast was buried in feet of snow, and the NY airports were all closed. Our flight east was canceled, not postponed. We compartmentalized the engagement ring issue, and did what we do best: the Sammis family adapted to new circumstances. We looked at the next couple days as a gift, a free period with no plans, no expectations. We explored, revisited my old haunts from when I met and married Mary in 1976 - 1978. I showed them my apartments

Scott meets the DeSantis family

in Haight Ashbury and Russian Hill, where Mary and I met. We rode cable cars, and had Irish coffee at the Buena Vista Cafe, the self-proclaimed inventor of the drink. We indulged ourselves in just being "the four of us." I think it reassured each of us that we had lost nothing, and that we would always have "us." On the fourth day we finally made it onto a flight, and flew back to miserable New York. We met Tina at JFK, I hugged the kids goodbye, and hopped immediately on a JetBlue flight to West Palm Beach to meet Dad and the family. I was exhausted, but so happy to meet the extended DeSantis family.

The plan was for me to go to Florida for Christmas, return to NY to collect Scott, and go back to the Sunshine State for New Years, so he could meet my big Italian family. Crazy I know, but this was our fast track first year together. Mother Nature had a few obstacles in store. December in NY is normally on the mild side, usually no snow. When I parked the Jetta in the JetBlue garage I didn't think to park under a roof or awning, but right out in the open. My flight home to NY was canceled due to mounds of snow dumped on the Northeast. I knew I needed to bring home a shovel and snow boots. Good luck locating these items in Palm Beach, Florida! My niece Amanda was not to be deterred. She was determined to find them, and she did! My boots were funny looking and my shovel flimsy, but I managed to tunnel my way to the car and out of the parking garage. In the process, the shovel broke, and I got totally soaked. When I got to 83 Wisconsin St., it was the same story. Another half hour wielding that broken shovel, and I made it past the front door. Whew.

From the snow storms to the emotional storms of 2011, here we come....

I was ecstatic to finally have Tina back in my arms again, even if it was in the middle of JFK airport in the midst of an historic snow storm. We were going to Florida (she was returning) to meet the big DeSantis clan. I had heard a million stories, and couldn't wait to match faces with impressions. Of course, JetBlue delayed our flight for 3+ hours without much information. We busied ourselves compiling our "slap list," comprised of miscreants we agreed needed to be whacked. To the obvious picks of the flight schedulers and secret keepers at JetBlue, Tina wanted to add all the people who voted for George Bush. If they voted for him twice, two slaps. We arrived in West Palm at 4am. struggled to an airport hotel, connected furiously, and collapsed for a few hours.

We spent New Years with the incomparable Olsen family, Tina's sister Nancy, Art Sr., Art Jr., Brian and Christopher. The guys in the group are self-professed "Florida rednecks," who enjoy hunting, fishing, Nascar, and quad four-wheeling in the wilderness out back of their property. The whole gang was there to meet the mysterious, heralded Scott. I felt like a rock star. Smiles so bright, hugs so heartfelt. I was immediately and thoroughly welcomed into the heart of Tina's extended family. It was touching and surprising. They were so welcoming that the boys took us out back on our own quad cycle to show us some midnight fun, and we got completely lost, wandering around, listening to the wild boars calling to each other. We found our way back to the house somehow. My DeSantis family adventure had begun.

CHAPTER 15. Reality Sets In

We came home from our successful New Years trip in Florida to the frozen tundra of New York. Long Beach was not much fun with two feet of snow clogging the tiny crowded streets.

The pictures of my time in Florida were posted on Facebook. One of the first phone calls I received in the New Year was from Jim. "Are you still wearing your engagement ring, or did you get engaged?" He saw the picture on Facebook. I planned to tell him, just not during Christmas. He was also giving me a hell of a hard time with the divorce papers. There were suicide threats mixed in with the nit picking over the way the contract read. I admitted to him "Yes, Jim, I was going to tell you, it just happened so fast." That phone call ended abruptly.

Jim had gotten into the habit of calling me on Fridays. I kept Scott apprised - I wanted no secrets with him. I would talk to Jim as a concerned and caring friend. It was part of my healing as well. Scott was completely understanding. He knew I had to grieve, and our situation was so unique. Scott was not threatened by my sadness over the ending of my marriage to Jim. We were both in counseling with Dee, an amazing and wise woman who helped us tremendously. Scott had met Dee after he lost Mary, and she was their family counselor for years.

In early January I received a scathing email from Jim that actually gave me a rash from the stress it brought on. The email, which I still have to this day as a reminder, was full of blame and finger pointing. Jim was desperately trying to place the blame solely on me for the destruction of our marriage. He went so far as to say that I must have started my affair with Scott before his started with Jody. What did that matter? It incensed me because I sat at home on Friday nights for over a year not restarting my life while Jim lied to me. I hoped for the best, wondering if I could save a sinking ship. There was a lot of hurt inside me that it was difficult to release, due to the distraction of my happiness with Scott. The hurt needed to be unleashed. There was a time I trusted Jim 100%. I knew he was flawed, but I thought his love for me would help him overcome the weaknesses. Jim made a very big mistake, and was desperately trying to make sense of it to all of us, especially himself.

I was never so lucky to have Dee in my life as at this time. We worked together, along with Scott, to help me finally let go.

My closest emotional adviser, apart from the kids and now Tina, was Dee my counselor who helped me rebuild my broken life after Mary died. I remember engaging with her six months after the accident. Dee got right to the point. "What are you *really* worried about?" I tried a few possible ideas, searching, and she smiled, rejected them all, and persisted. Finally, a lump grew in my throat. "I'm worried that if I don't come to grips with this horror, I will crawl into an emotional fetal position, and never be able to find another soul mate." Dee smiled and whispered "there it is. Now let's get to work."

Dee guided me through my multiple simultaneous role changes. The accident had moved me from husband to widower, the business sale had ushered me from business owner to semi-retiree, my dad's death in 2007 after mom's in 1998 turned me from son to "orphan", and the kids growing up pushed me from full time dad to long distance cheerleader. I grew to respect Dee's sage advice and deft ability to draw out my true feelings. She was very excited about my second chance with Tina, but she anticipated trouble if Tina wasn't afforded the time to "process" her feelings of loss about her marriage to Jim. In Dee's view this would entail several months of time alone for Tina. I despised the idea of being apart from Tina, mostly because I needed to see her so badly, but partly for fear I would lose her to someone else. She hadn't been "on the market" for even a nanosecond after her marriage ended, and I knew the suitors were lined up. Still, Dee knew her stuff, and I was aware of my proclivity to push too hard, too fast, to be impetuous and impatient. The last thing I wanted to do was suffocate Tina, delay her grieving over the lost marriage, only to have it erupt later down the line.

I struggled with this conundrum. As January progressed into February Tina and I started to discuss what should happen when her lease ran out in May on 83 Wisconsin St. It was our love nest, where we really caught fire, a magical launching pad for this romantic rocket. I had a beautiful home I wanted to share with her, and I wanted us to be permanently linked. But Dee words rang in my ears. "You must give her time to process, alone." I wanted the honeymoon to be a reality, NOW. Tina and Jim were fighting and crying. It broke my heart to see her struggle. He infuriated her, but mostly she felt so sorry. She desperately did not want to hurt him. What to do?

Resolution came naturally. Dee started to see Tina with me. It became clear to her that Tina and I were like a force of nature, undeniable. We realized we "should" be apart for awhile, but neither one of could stand the idea. There was simply no way. In a short while, Dee blessed our impetuous fast track plan.

CHAPTER 16. New Zealand

Tina discovered we were trekking to New Zealand at our first date at Fat Fish last summer. That trip was approaching in February, but first I needed to take Tina to Caneel Bay in St. John, Virgin Islands to escape the horrific NY January winter. I had been camping in Cinnamon Bay campground 30 years earlier, but never to a place like Caneel. Tina was giddy, love drunk again, but Jim's emotional outbursts were taking their toll on her. She loved the Caribbean, but her skin did not. A little overexposure to the direct St. John sun the first day, her sensitive epidermis, and the low-grade emotional fever she got processing her feelings about Jim all conspired to create quite an aggressive skin rash. Not too painful, but the poor girl had red bumps everywhere and white, ivy-looking patches on her back. Apart from the skin eruptions, we slept late, explored the garden island in a rented jeep, and enjoyed champagne dinners outside. Too soon we headed back to New York, and her skin returned to normal.

My niece Stephanie, my best friend, was preparing to marry the man of her dreams, Steve, in magical New Zealand where he was born and raised. Scott made this trip possible for me, and we were thrilled to be going halfway around the planet. Scott had been to NZ before, and advised me it may be the most beautiful and mystical place on the earth. I had not traveled much except for our annual Caribbean vacation with Jim. New Zealand seemed like a fairy tale, a world away, and it was.

At the time my job was very demanding, but I had a competent assistant Kristen who assured me she'd be OK for two weeks without me. My immediate supervisor gave me a very difficult time. The day we were leaving from JFK midday I came to work in jeans, so Scott could pick me up on the way. My boss sent me home, like a school girl breaking the dress code. I was distraught with anger and stress. Remember, they had aggressively and relentlessly recruited me when I was with Scott's company, put me in a big office with tons of responsibility, and demanded a lot. I rose to the occasion. But here I was being punished and humiliated like a child. My supervisor was a small minded individual. Because of this trip and my relationship with Scott, he figured I would no longer need this job, and would be quitting soon. I had no such intentions. I wanted to keep this big job for as long as I could. The mistreatment sent me off on my journey full of worry. Would I have a job when I returned?

After dropping Tina off at her office the morning we were leaving - I would be grabbing her in a few hours to catch an afternoon flight to NZ - I flipped on WCBS 880 AM radio. Top of the hour came breathless reports of an earthquake in the capital city of New Zealand, Christ Church., on the south island. We were to land there, and then go to the north island for the wedding. I called Air New Zealand immediately, expecting bad news. Nope. They had heard nothing. Then came the phone call from Tina. Her bosses had "sent her home" for a wardrobe infraction. How ridiculous and insulting. They had apparently concluded she didn't need the job, having married an insurance agent who had recently sold his business, and would leave them soon. They lashed out first. Very mature.

New Zealand was everything Scott said it would be - paradise. Stephanie and Steve's wedding was something out of a fairly tale. Palm trees, gentle breezes, azure waters, deep blue skies. On the ferry ride over to the wedding island reception, dolphins followed our boat.

Scott & Tina in NZ

Tina and I took every opportunity to experience New Zealand, kayaking Milford Sound in high winds, horseback riding the routes taken in the recent filming of Lord of the Rings, zip lining across a river, and walking everywhere. She was able to forget her work issue temporarily, but I knew it was always in the back of her mind. Meanwhile, I had invested heavily in the precious metal silver over the past five years, and was watching open-mouthed, as the price rose from $18 per ounce in September 2010 to $50 by April 2011. What possibilities. Life was good.

CHAPTER 17. Moving In/ Tough Transitions

By the spring I was talking to Dee with Scott, and she agreed we needed to be together, and shouldn't wait. She did, however, suggest that we get a place of our own, to start fresh. Scott was not on board with the idea. He knew well the pains of moving, and strongly opposed it. He was hopeful that our transition to living together in 28 Flower Hill would be smooth. Not.

I moved in early April of 2011. Becky and her boyfriend (now hubby) Shawn helped us get my belongings from Long Beach to Huntington. They joked that I had a bowling ball, recalling my turn as ringer at Thanksgiving, and said they loved Long Beach, wishing they could have spent more time there with us. Scott had made some room for me in Mary's old closet, but it was very difficult for me as there were still some of her stuff in there. There were also pictures of their lives together on every wall and every corner, constant reminders to me that this wasn't a home I created. All these things, along with a house full of clutter and disarray, made me disinclined to leave my apartment.

Scott and I did not spend much time in Huntington. We were mostly in Long Beach. I failed to absorb all that was *awaiting me in this new home.*

I worked closely with Dee during this time. She worked with me to find my voice. At this point, things were moving so fast, however, and I underestimated the many hurdles we had ahead of us.

A wedding date was set for September 9, 2011. I wasn't divorced, and now I found myself living in a home I was extremely uncomfortable in. Scott and I had our little bubble house in Long Beach. I wanted to stay there.

I wasn't aware of how the kids were so affected by our quick decisions, nor could I begin to understand the enormity of pain they felt from losing their mom so suddenly. They were petrified of losing their dad. They didn't know me. I loved them, and wanted them to be a part of our lives. I wanted to start fresh, and hoped they did as well, but they seemed resistant to our changes.

Scott was ready to start anew, and he and I were completely on the same page when it came to de-cluttering and redecorating and making the house our own. So we started.

We had some decisions to make. First was do we stay at 83 Wisconsin Street until the end of the lease? This would afford Tina a little more emotional breathing room, but require me to make the 1 hour/trip commute 10 times a week. Or do we take the plunge and move to 28 Flower Hill? The

$2000 monthly rent was a concern also. In the end, patience did not carry the day: we decided to move in to the big house. Dee cautioned us how difficult it would be, with memories, "ghosts," kids still in residence, etc. She said we should get our own home, start fresh, avoid the coming anxieties. I tried to be comfortable with the idea, but I simply couldn't face putting myself and the kids through the emotional turmoil. I was hopeful (naively) that everyone would adapt to the wonderful change and, most importantly, Tina would feel "at home." I needed her with me. I was willing to change virtually everything in the house, including the paint and furniture, to make it new. Sounded simple. As it turned out, the process of integrating Tina into the family was much more laborious, painful and difficult by moving in to 28 Flower Hill than I could have imagined. I should have apologized to everyone for my stubbornness and naivete.

The other decision was how long to hang on to the September marriage date at Raphael Winery. I urgently wanted to marry Tina, but three things troubled me. One was the fact that the Friday date would preclude many of our work friends from participating. Two was my nagging feeling that I was forcing the issue and acting too much like my narcissistic dad Quentin, who selfishly advanced his own wedding date with my mother by several months to February 1950. This meant her family from Wisconsin family could not attend. Third was the messy reality that the lawyers involved in Tina's divorce were making little to no progress. Would Tina even be able to marry legally in September? For these reasons, we abandoned the Friday date and rescheduled for May 19, 2012, a Saturday. Ever the impatient one, I proposed a new plan. Why not get married "secretly" in Woodstock, NY by my son John, an officiant in the Universal Life Church (of the Internet) on October 1, 2011? We could preserve the May 19th date for Tina's dad to walk her down the aisle, and for the gathering of the two extended families. We decided to go for it!

We had so much fun picking out paint colors and new furniture for 28 Flower Hill Road. Our tastes were so similar. We love the coastal feel and chose some beautiful coastal colors and furnishings. Scott's son John was not so favorable. When Mary passed, Scott and the kids hung on to each other for dear life. Not having experienced such loss, I did not understand their fear and resistance to change. Instead of understanding, I took it all too personally. I felt like shutting down. These were difficult times, and I wanted to run. I thought "this is not what I signed up for." But I didn't run. I loved Scott more that I'd ever loved before. I knew I just had to figure it out.

Scott and I talked about this situation constantly. We continued counseling, and forged forward. Scott urged me to be patient, "things were improving." Trevor was living on his own in DC, Becky was moving in with her boyfriend, and John had an apartment in Port Jefferson where he was attending *SUNY Stony Brook* trying to get into medical school. There was progress. But these were still some of the roughest months I went through. I tried to be gentle with them, remembering what they must have gone through losing their mom.

CHAPTER 18. Divorces and Weddings

We broached the idea of our intimate Woodstock wedding to Trevor, Becky and John in the summer, and they enthusiastically embraced it. I rented four rooms at the Wild Rose Inn. We arranged to have tuxedo t shirts made up and pink feather boas collected. I wrote my vows. They came easily. I was so ready. Tina was consumed with an increasingly contentious work environment and struggling to make 28 Flower Hill Road her own. She would need to take a "me weekend" to write her vows in September. She booked a room at Gurney's in Montauk.

On a quick August weekend trip to the Woodstock area to see friends we were treated to quite a surprise. We stayed in the cute village of Phoenicia, home to Sweet Sue's famous breakfast restaurant. After visiting the friends we ate dinner at Ricardelli's in Phoenicia. Adele's song "Someone like you" came over the music system, and the bottled up emotions in me burst into tears. All the turmoil in Huntington, my unfinished feelings of grieving for my marriage, plus the news I'd gotten the day before that the divorce was final, combined to wash over me. Scott had an inkling of what it was about, but I just sniffled "I'm OK," and we finished dinner.

The next day we got up late and headed over to Sweet Sue's for brunch. The hostess sat us at a table for two by the front window, overlooking the street and the walkway up to the cafe. As I was trying to decide what to have, I looked up from the menu, and Scott's eyes were bulging. "You're NOT going to believe who is walking into the restaurant right now." I turned to the front door just as my ex Jim and girlfriend Jodi were making their way in. I was stunned, as was Jim. Jodi and Scott seemed to disappear, I think he went to the bathroom. I had been here with Jim numerous times in our marriage, so it seemed strangely normal to be exchanging pleasantries with him here now. He was reserved, I guessed from hearing the news of the divorce yesterday. Scott reappeared, so we all smiled and went our separate ways. I know I appeared the calmest of all four, but the chance meeting rattled me. On the drive home, we stopped at a funeral for the brother of one of my friends. After another crying jag, I felt tired, but relieved, like I had let a lot of emotion go and been cleared out. I looked over at Scott driving the car. He didn't know what hit him this weekend.

Wow. All I could think as I saw Jim and Jodi striding up the walk to Sweet Sue's was the Bogart "Casablanca" line "of all the gin joints in all the world, you had to walk into mine." After I shook Jim's hand and introduced myself to Jodi, I could tell where she wanted to be: ANY OTHER RESTAURANT IN THE WORLD. Tina comes up big in difficult social situations. She sorted out who arrived when, where was everyone staying, etc. When I got back from the bathroom, it was all over. I asked Tina "are you OK?" She looked at her food and said "Let's eat our eggs, and get the hell out of here." After all the challenges and crying, the takeaway from the weekend was we were free to get married in October!

The secret 10/1/11 wedding date was quickly approaching. We wanted to preserve the big formal wedding date of May 19th to have my dad walk me down the aisle. I knew he'd be so proud. This October subterfuge was in true Scott fashion – he couldn't wait to be married. But it was painful for me. I really wanted my sisters at the October event, but realized that the cat would get out of the bag, and Dad would hear about it. We decided to keep it from my sisters. How do you think that worked out?

My part in keeping the October wedding secret from Tina's sisters was to go to the barbecue at ToniAnne's the weekend Tina was at Gurney's, and lie. When I showed up alone, and told them she had a reunion to attend, it went over like a lead balloon. NOBODY believed it. I could tell Toni's antenna was up, and Nancy would soon be consulted.

The weekend before the secret wedding in Woodstock ironically was Jim's birthday. I decided I needed a weekend away to write my vows, and sort out all that had occurred in the last few months. There was no doubl about being with

Scott, but I needed quiet and peaceful surroundings to clear my head. I decided to rent a suite at Gurney's Inn in Montauk, a picturesque seaside resort that quiets down in the fall. When I lied to my sisters about my whereabouts this particular weekend, their antennas went up like Russian spies. My phone did not stop. My sister Nancy went so far as to plead with me "not to hurt Scott!" They thought I was on a secret rendezvous with Jim for his birthday! Nothing could have been further from the truth.

I wrote my vows on a sunny Saturday afternoon, sitting bundled up on a beach chair with a warm cup of coffee. They flowed from my pen with an ease I've never felt before. I was ready. I knew I had to confess to my sisters and explain why I did what I did. They understood, stopped being mad at me. They were still my beautiful bridesmaids in May!

The original September Friday wedding did not take place, but the "secret" October one did! Tina will tell you we married early "for insurance purposes," because my 18 month COBRA health care coverage ran out 10/1. I still believe I (we?) just could not wait to be married. As it turned out, I am just as impatient as my father was.

We all arrived at Wild Rose in a joyful and rambunctious mood. Becky brought her husband to be (they weren't engaged yet) Shawn, who we loved. John brought his new flame Bonny who was fun and we hoped would work out (it did!). Only Trevor came solo. He was disengaging from a long relationship, and felt better on his own. He was happy to be there. We all enjoyed a raucous night in Woodstock the last day of September. The first of October arrived, and we all

Bride Tina at Wild Rose Inn

suited up at the Wild Rose. Tina was resplendent in an antique wedding veil and pink boa. We all trooped up to Overlook Mountain trail, about an hour up a fairly steep grade.

Panting, we arrived at our wedding venue, the ruins of an old 1928 Catskills mountain resort. With my beloved children all around us, we exchanged vows, everyone giddy at the spectacle. Officiant John pronounced us man and wife, and the champagne cork popped. I remember smiling so hard my cheeks hurt. Almost 70 months after a tragedy ripped our little family apart, my dream was coming true, I was married to my soul mate, a lot of

Cork Popping

healing had occurred, our group of four was now five, on its way to eight (seven were present now). What a blissfully hopeful moment. We then stomped back down the trail and re-adjourned in front of the fireplace at Wild Rose to create some classic wedding pictures. The wedding revelry began. So did the 40 year honeymoon. Unofficially.

CHAPTER 19. The Dreaded Holidays

How do you blend four different families together during the holidays? You don't. Some powerful lessons were learned this month of December 2011. In my line of work - contractor insurance - December is called Hell Month. I was responsible for four $1,000,000 clients whose coverage programs renewed on January 1. For me, this meant long hours in the office preparing and negotiating, as well as intense travel to clients' offices. It was next to impossible for me to take any time off in the month of December. The retention of these account fell on my shoulders.

The Sammis kids looked forward to their California family Christmas tradition all year - it was their way to reconnect with their mom, and be with their aunts and cousins whom they love, and have deep connections with. I wanted to please them, and make sure Scott was with his children on this holiday trip. The year prior we were engaged and spent the holidays apart. I knew if I didn't go to California Scott would not go, and the children would miss their dad's presence. I agreed to go to CA with my new family. Mind you, my family were not too thrilled about losing me, but completely understood.

Since my mother's passing in 1998 my oldest sister Tonianne continued our Christmas tradition. Her home was open to all, warm and delightful. Toni and I would gather a week prior to Christmas and make the traditional manicotti shells from scratch, drink red wine, and listen to Jerry Vale, our mother's favorite Italian singer. Christmas day was full of friends, family and people who did not have a place to go. My mother never wanted anyone to be alone on the holidays. My sister carried her sentiments. It was hard for me that my new step kids did not want to share in my tradition. It was an impossible situation.

As the pre-holiday days passed, and my nights in the office grew longer and longer, I realized that if I wanted to keep my job and my accounts, I absolutely could NOT take any days off. I had a huge decision to make. I was not ready to lose this position. I told Scott one evening in bed that I had to pull out of the CA trip, but wanted him to go. He sat up in bed immediately with conviction in his voice, "absolutely NOT! I will not leave you alone on Christmas, the kids are adults and will understand." I begged, pleaded and cried for him to go. He was adamant. I knew deep in my gut that the kids would NOT understand, they would not be kind, and would hold me responsible. I felt their sorrow and their anger. I knew there was trouble and pain ahead.

Scott canceled both our plane reservations under serious resistance from me. We experienced our first major blowout fight. I demanded that he go to California with the kids. If he didn't, I would leave the relationship.

I tried so hard to be honest with my step kids. I told them I could not go, and why, as well, I wanted badly for their dad to go with them. I'm not sure they believed me. But Scott believed I would leave if he did not reverse the cancellation and accompany his kids. So he went back to American Airlines, feeling defeated, and re-booked his flight without me. I was relieved and hoped my step kids were comforted that their dad would be with them. This selfless act backfired. I was alone Christmas morning texting my step kids, hoping they were enjoying their CA family, telling then I missed them, and sending them love. What I received was radio silence. Scott and I missed each other terribly. It turned out the kids wanted what they wanted, for us all to be together in California. Their inability to see my dilemma hurt me deeply.

One of the lessons Scott and I learned was that, when we had the chance to bail out on the CA trip in the fall, we should have taken it. We broached the idea of passing on the trip and were met with a threat. "If you don't come to California, the entire family out there won't come to your wedding in May!" The threat stunned me and I faltered, agreeing to go. In retrospect we should have taken the threat, given them love, and told them we would always be there for them, but stood our ground that Christmas in CA *might have to change for us. We needed to make our own traditions.*

Since Mary died, the children and I had made our way out to California to be with her family: Mary's three sisters, one of her two brothers, spouses, eleven cousins, and assorted heart mates. The first few years we rented big rambling houses in Santa Barbara and Santa Cruz, and camped out. The kids immersed themselves in hilarious testosterone games like "Bean bomb farfagnugen" (there were eight male cousins, all 20-something), boardgames and general horseplay. I hung out with the adults to the extent I could. Mostly I went to bed early, got up before dawn, grabbed a Starbucks, and watched the sunrise on the Pacific. I missed Mary ferociously. The kids processed the loss more privately. We were on different pages in that regard, but we needed to be in the same place together.

Our Sammis family Huntington Christmas tradition was more harrowing than most in the years before Mary's passing, principally because we were impelled into the midst of my parents' miserable marriage, debilitating divorce, and awful alimony period, lasting altogether fifteen plus years. They lived five minutes from each other and five minutes from us, they knew all the same people, and I worked closely with my father throughout. As my uncle Gordon once quipped "son, your situation is untenable." He was right. We saw both of my parents each at Christmas, exchanged gifts and pretended not to notice the grab bag of toxic emotions surrounding the holiday. For her part, Mary was as gracious as she could be. Her stress came out in decorating for the holidays. If the kids and I weren't diligent or enthusiastic enough about hauling the house decorations up from the basement, she became sulky, and snapped at us. Same with undecorating. I really can't blame her. She didn't sign up for this persistent family dysfunction. We did manage to carve out a little chunk of happiness for the five of us. We opened presents early on Christmas Day, reveled in hugs and silly pictures, made scrambled eggs and toast for breakfast, and took a brisk cold walk with Niko, our golden retriever, out at Asharoken Beach or Caumsett Park. It was our small slice of tradition.

As the 2011 holiday approached, Tina and the kids were getting along famously. We all felt great about the secret wedding ceremony up at Woodstock, and were anticipating the journey together to CA to be with Mary's family. Then some threads of the good feeling tapestry started to unravel, and the slow motion train wreck began. Tina so wanted to please the kids that she said she "really wanted to go to California." I knew that wasn't a firm commitment, and sure enough, as the days grew shorter and her work days became longer and more pressurized, I could see we were heading for trouble. We made plane reservations. By mid-December it was clear Tina was in a furious battle to retain her most important accounts at work. I knew the business, and it appeared to me to be like hand to hand combat. Something had to give. We told the kids we couldn't make it to CA. I canceled the plane reservations. My reasoning was my life had changed, I was married now, and I wanted to be with my new wife on our first married Christmas. Trevor, Becky and John despised the change in plans. They went silent.

It turns out Tina hated the idea of me skipping CA also. She felt so terrible about not going she was determined not to "ruin the kids' Christmas." They needed their dad. Not thinking about herself, or me, or us, she was adamant that I go. I refused. We commenced perhaps the blackest, dirtiest fight we'd experienced. Both of us dug in. What sealed it for me was this statement from Tina: "If you don't go to California with your kids, I'm not sure I know who you are. And I don't know if I can be with someone I don't know." Snap. That did it. My buttons were pushed simultaneously. I slammed down the phone, called the airline to resuscitate my reservation, and flew to California.

As I boarded the flight to CA I was furious with Tina *and* my kids. I knew in my heart I should be with her, but she had just dropped some relationship threatening bombs, and I hit the roof. My children earned my ire for refusing to be understanding of my need to be with my new mate. I certainly did not understand how frightened they were of "losing" their dad this close in time to the loss of their mom. They thought the worst was happening, and they just wanted us all to be in California TOGETHER. It was impossible situation that exploded, leaving all of us wounded.

After a day or two of sulking in CA, I began to call Tina incessantly. Of course, the cell service in the tiny town of Amador, CA is abysmal. My heart certainly wasn't in the West coast family reunion. I spent a lot of time alone, wanting to be back East. Tina spent Christmas Eve alone in 28 Flower Hill Road with Niko and her two cats, Preston and Pierre. We both blew it. I came home as soon as we could, and Tina and I started to heal.

CHAPTER 20. Blowing it Up/ Talking it Out

One thing that made it through the Holiday successfully was my professional career. We kept all the critical account renewals, and in January I received a lofty Christmas bonus. I decided to treat Scott and myself to two nights in January at the iconic Plaza Hotel in Manhattan. A new shared passion for us was to walk around NYC. We loved the smells, sights and magic of the big bustling city.

Our favorite time in our new honeymoon is "bubble time," when it's just the two of us, and our favorite place is strolling places like Central Park in New York. We often fantasized about a weekend in the fabled Plaza Hotel, right on Central Park South. For Christmas Tina splurged some of her hard-earned bonus money on a long weekend for us at the Plaza. As we drove into the city that Friday afternoon with plans in our heads and romance in our eyes, Tina started to worry about the condition of the house upon our return, if the kids decided to party. The house was newly decorated, much less cluttered, and well-organized. The kids knew, if a party were to occur, the house would need to be restored to order before we got back. This was discussed and understood. I urged her not to anticipate trouble. She agreed, and we happily checked in to the Plaza.

It was a freezing weather weekend, but our hearts were warm. Our wedding-for-real was coming up in four months time, and we had been diligently preparing our wedding waltz at Arthur Murray twice a week for several months already. We were pretty good. We found ourselves humming the hauntingly beautiful wedding song "Open Arms" by Journey as we swooped through Walmart parking lots, Manhattan sidewalks, and Central Park. We got a lot of puzzled looks, some stares, but mostly smiles from the onlookers. We visited the Natural History Museum and chuckled at the brain display of the amygdala, our "reptile brain," which we reckoned caused most of our frightened, insecure, and vulnerable feelings, always trying to warn the rest of the brain of all the horrible threats out there. We likened the amygdala to our little internal selves, "little Tina" and "little Scott," constantly on guard against pain-causing situations they could relate to from childhood. We were getting accomplished at talking through these awkward situations, and not placing bricks. We danced at Swing 46 Club and dined elegantly. The weekend was nearly perfect.

We had been waiting for a call from John to let us know he had been accepted into New York College of Osteopathic Medicine, NYCOM. He finally called and gave us the news he MADE IT! What an achievement! He was a late bloomer who decided late to be a doctor, had worked his butt off, and was making his dream happen. My heart overflowed with pride. After a beat, he asked "do you mind if I have a few people over to celebrate?" It was true that, throughout their teen years, Mary and I had allowed 28 Flower Hill Road to be the gathering house, the "party house." The strict rules were understood and enforced: no drinking in the house, keys collected, no one drives inebriated, they could always sleep at 28 FH. After Mary died I didn't discourage them from using the house. Right now this seemed a little short-sighted. I said yes to the gathering, but Tina and I both felt a sense of dread. We drove home not knowing what to expect.

It had become a pattern with the step kids to have parties in our home when we went out or were away. I was growing tired of it. They were no longer teens. They were 27, 29, and 32. Although we were getting to know each other and opening up more, there were resentments about what happened during the holidays and more brewing about how Scott and I were making the house our own. In the process of transforming the living room with paint, decorations and furniture, we considered getting rid of the small piano that was never used any more. Upon hearing that, John pronounced we would jettison the piano "over my dead body." Wow, he wasn't kidding. We had struck some kind of nerve. I took note. That comment was very upsetting for both of us.

After we heard the news Saturday that John was accepted to NYCOM, Scott had agreed to make the house available for a small celebration. On the drive home from the Plaza we fell silent, equal parts hoping the clean up crew had finished, and dreading that they hadn't. I had a gnawing feeling that our home would be a wreck when we arrived. John has asked to have "a few people over." We were so happy for him, but I knew his patterns, and the partying was bad. We walked in through the garage door, and I could feel the panic in the house. It was turned upside down. Pizza boxes were piled high, empty bottles of beer and wine were strewn about, half eaten pizza on plates all over. Pictures were removed from the walls. What the hell? It was 3 o'clock in the afternoon, and they were just starting to straighten up. They seemed still drunk from the night before. I lost it. I went upstairs, changed my clothes, and left without saying a word. I wanted to run as far away as possible. My head was in a terrible place. I knew I had to confront this issue head on, or my marriage to Scott could not last. After I calmed down a bit, I texted the kids to apologize for storming out, and asked for us all to meet.

As Tina stormed out I was overcome by emotion. The nasty thought popped up that John had dragged his feet on cleaning up on purpose to make a passive-aggressive point about this being HIS house too. That pissed me off, but I dismissed it. I was deeply disappointed the kids would be so inconsiderate. And seriously worried if Tina and I would be able to work this out. I had completely underestimated the level of resistance there would be to us becoming a warm, new family. Things were bad, real bad. The kids' anger and hurt were deeply felt, and so were Tina's and mine, all for different reasons. We all felt threatened, insecure and vulnerable, a regular amygdala overload. I was still hopeful, knowing how well-meaning and wonderful each of us was individually, that we could grow to be that happy trusting family, but that hope was just a glimmer now. We needed to have it out, air our grievances, speak our truths, and clear up some misunderstandings. After all, we each had a stake in rebuilding this family. It was unclear to me how that would happen. We shuffled around the kitchen making order out of chaos. Tina was the first to storm off, but she's also very examined and sensitive. She did what she always does. She texted us all, said she was sorry and really cared, and could we all meet in the kitchen of 28 Flower Hill in a few days to figure out what just happened? We put the last plate and pizza box away, took a big breath and agreed to the pow wow in a few days.

We agreed to a family dinner meeting at 28 Flower Hill. Myself, Scott, Becky and John. Trevor lived in Philadelphia at the time, and couldn't make the meeting. John started off strong. He came at us with "I've fucking had it." Immediately I felt threatened, and started to shake a little. What the hell could this 27 year old have "had it" with? Being asked not to trash our home? There was so much anger inside him that I soon felt I was not dealing with a 27 year old ,but someone who had been dealing with a lot more than not being allowed to have a house party.

I tried to reason with him, but I was getting angrier and angrier. At one point my run response kicked in and I spit out "I'm DONE!," and turned to walk out. Up until now, Becky had been listening to John and me go at it, but she grabbed by arm, blocked my progress, and said "you're not leaving us." Looking back at it now, Becky single handedly saved us. She remains an incredibly fair minded and sane part of our wild family. She sees all sides, and tries to help us do the same.

I sat back down. Scott and Becky had been quiet so far, now it was my turn. Becky was there for her brother, explaining his worries that we were re-decorating and taking down his childhood memories. My heart broke. But I needed him to see that his future was so bright, and his dad and I needed a fresh start as well. My response to him was rational. I told him that he wasn't a child anymore, that, at 27, he soon would be getting a home with his then serious girlfriend (now wife), and I wouldn't expect them to let me in to decorate. His next complaint was no pictures of his mom were in the house. That wasn't entirely true, but there were fewer showing than before. We had been very slow to put up new pictures. I asked John to pick out some pictures he wanted and we would hang them. I went so far as finding several pictures of John and his mom, but he never chose them to put up.

Becky's complaints were a little less petulant. She thought I really didn't want to go to CA for Christmas and was lying, trying to accommodate them. She was half right. I did want to please them. I would have gone as a family, if I weren't seriously worried about losing my job. They did not understand my position at work. I could not expect them to. They grew up very differently than I did. It was hard for us all to see the other side.

We made it through the meeting. In the middle, John broke down into uncontrollable sobs, as did Scott and Becky. Scott felt horrible that he did not see this brewing. The kids were afraid of losing him. He assured them that COULD NEVER HAPPEN. I assured them I could never be a part of that. I asked John if I could come over and hug him while he was sobbing, and he told me that was a wonderful idea. We hugged and cried and came to a special place. The long and arduous healing process had begun.

I was very proud of all of us, four worthy people under great duress, threatened, scared, but willing to be vulnerable, and search for understanding. Here with me were three of the most important people in the world to me, all in pain. At the beginning of the meeting I was overwhelmed, so I took a back seat, listening to those more in touch with their feelings. John had started off aggressively defending his ownership of his childhood home, and attacking Tina and me for changing it physically and behaviorally. Tina defended herself vigorously, not wanting to draw blood, but was hurt herself. Becky was worried that Tina was less than truthful about really wanting to be with them in California. I was rocked by the power of all this emotion in the people I loved, and I broke down at the end of the meeting. The thought that I had somehow caused this misery was too much to take. Hugs and more tears brought us all together.

The kitchen confrontation was cathartic, but did not bring resolution. There was much more ground to cover. Becky and John discussed the meeting with Trevor, and they all decided it was time for a family intervention with me, facilitated by Dee, our family counselor. All of us had spoken with Dee over the last five years, although none so intensely as me. They all respected her guidance and insight, but each possessed varying degrees of desire or courage to engage with her consistently. After Kilimanjaro I felt in my bones they all needed help out of the blackness. They all resisted, fearful they said of "going back there" to the bad periods. John and Becky called them "freakouts," in which they would sob uncontrollably. I was desperate, in the early years, to impel them into talking with her, to feel the healing that I experienced. When I expressed my frustration to Dee, she said you have two choices: either keep hounding them until they freeze you out completely, or shut up, continue your own healing, thereby leading them to happiness, by example. I shut up. My ongoing inability to connect with them to share the misery, commiserate and cry together was a source of sadness for me.

Trevor, Becky, John and I gathered at Dee's house in various states of anxiety. I had only a vague idea of what issues they would bring. It was their show. John was the most hurt by the dispossession of 28 Flower Hill, but Trevor took the lead. He had left the house for college after only six years at that house, and never really returned for more than a summer. Becky had a big group of friends over frequently for the nine years she lived at 28 FH. John's friends were there for 11 years. The changes in décor upset them, especially the disappearance of all the Mary pictures I displayed after her death. Dee asked gently if Tina and I had a right to make changes there? They acquiesced. After a rambling discussion, Becky offered "look, guys, the way to understand this is, 28 Flower Hill Road is our *house,* but it's not *our* house anymore." Bittersweet, but true. Tina wasn't invited to this intervention, because they all wanted to express their fear of losing me. That was a frustration for me. I felt zero diminution in my love for them, so in my gut I didn't know what they were worried about. In fact I was upset and disappointed they doubted the deepest depth of my love for them. For me that was like a rock, permanent and unchanging. I would do anything for them, always. What part of that did they not understand? My love for Tina would ADD to my capacity to love them, not dilute it.

What I did realize was that little Trevor, little Becky and little John were petrified they would lose the only parent they had left. They felt Tina had captured the heart of their dad, and he would marginalize his kids. I said "if anything I love you *more* than before Tina came into my life. Here is when I stop loving you: NEVER. We are 'the four of us,' did you forget? You will NEVER lose me, EVER. All I've done here is bring another amazing person into the group to double the love we shower on you. I ask you for only one thing: do not suffer or stew over this 'losing Dad' thing. If it pops up in your head, you *call me* instantly, you hear? I love you ferociously. I have your back. I am the main person in your corner. That will never change!" By that point, even Dee was crying. I guess they really needed to hear all that, huh?

Immediately after the intervention we went to meet Tina, to include her in the healing process. Becky had been nervous about excluding her, so we all agreed to meet right after.

I was very nervous about the family of four meeting with Dee. I wasn't invited, but totally understood - the kids needed their Dad's undivided attention. They asked me to meet them for dinner after. The two hours seemed like eight. I knew there were more issues after our Kitchen table discussion, but it was so hard for me to imagine what they were. Scott called me immediately after the session with Dee ended. He advised me it went amazingly. I walked into their favorite family hibachi joint. Becky greeted me with a big smile, saying "you, you were voted off the island." I laughed and hugged her. She told me I should have been there. At dinner we didn't speak of what happened at Dee's. Scott brought me up to speed later in private. I've learned so many things this first year with my Sammis family. The first is "kids don't come with an operating manual," Scott's famous saying. There are all levels of healing. I'm ever so grateful that I have these Sammis kids in my life. The lessons they've taught me about unconditional love and fear are priceless. We were ready now to get going on that May wedding.

CHAPTER 21. Let the Healing Begin

Two important dates were quickly approaching: Scott's 60th birthday and our May wedding at the vineyard. I did not want this milestone birthday to get trumped because of our upcoming wedding. Scott does so much for so many, he deserved a celebration, and I was determined to make this a birthday he would remember, feel special about, and realize how important he is to all of us. I've heard him mention in passing that the parties he's had at "big" birthdays, ie. 40th, 50th, etc., he planned himself. I wanted to put an end to that!!

The kids and I plotted quietly. We knew we had to tell him we were going to do "something," otherwise he would know something was up. So I told him I was going to rent two hotel suites in New York City, for us and for the kids, and we would go to a play the next day. Scott was thrilled and humble. I told him to just relax. He was knee deep in wedding preparations, making lists, getting nervous about lodging all the out of towners, and how our wedding day was going to pan out.

The run up to the wedding was intense, with so many decisions to make. We made all the meetings and judgments together, but as the time shortened, two things happened: one, Tina started to hyperventilate, and I lost confidence in the wedding venue planners. At a meeting out at the vineyard where they mount dozens and dozens of weddings each year, they showed us a table plan that had the wrong number of tables and seats. Tina was already anticipating armageddon, so I made a decision: I will take over the planning from here. I will manage the guest list, the lodging arrangements, and prepare marching orders for each participant in the production. I ordered Tina to stop worrying, and focus on her own beautification. To my amazement, she complied. She let me take charge. That's when I stopped sleeping...

I started calling Scott "groomzilla," when it came to the wedding preparations, but I didn't want him to worry about what to do for his birthday. I guess it worked out he was so preoccupied with orchestrating the movements of 150 friends and relatives over a May weekend, he didn't think about his 60th. In the background, the kids and I were secretly gathering some of Scott's closest and dearest comrades for a surprise dinner in Manhattan. The play was just a decoy. We collected his closest friend Fred and his lovely wife Pat, some of his dear friends at the YMCA, as well as "the Marys" who were his wife's closest hiking buddies. These ladies were a huge part of the Sammis' lives, and I wanted them to continue to be in our lives. They are lovely, warm and have welcomed me with open arms and hearts. We had our plan in place with all the players. My sister Tonianne and husband Dick were part of the posse as well. All were huge fans of my amazingly wonderful husband.

Perfect crowd to celebrate this man.

I rented a private room at a fun and lively Cuban restaurant called Dos Caminos right down the block from the hotel. After a long day walking around Central Park, enjoying the sights with the kids, practicing our wedding waltz while Trevor took cell phone videos, we were ready to go to our hotel rooms and prepare for dinner and our surprise!!

We got to the restaurant, and the hostess led us to the table. All of our loved ones were there and yelled "SURPRISE!!" Scott looked around and was wondering why all these people that he loved and knew were in the same room yelling surprise. When he figured it out, he hugged and kissed me. I believe that was one of the happiest faces I'd seen in quite a while. We needed this gathering, we needed to celebrate this man, we needed to go forward as a family.

CHAPTER 22. Wedding Preparation

From the minute I laid eyes on Tina under the dome at 125 Froehlich Farm Boulevard on December 8, 2008, I knew I would spend my life with her. With all the twists and turns of our messy lives I didn't *say* we'd be married until May of 2010. It took my mouth seventeen months to catch up with my heart. Our being together seemed so obvious and simple to me at first. We needed patience, fortitude, courage, luck, advice, love, understanding and an unbreakable connection to make this dream come true. Finally, 41 months after we met, realizing we were already married in the eyes of the law (and the insurance companies), we were going to tie the Big Knot. Tina's father Nick was going to walk his baby daughter down the aisle at Raphael Vineyard on May 19, 2012.

As we started the planning process, I felt a big wedding was never a dream for me. I grew up in a modest home, and financially it was never an option. Honestly I wasn't the typical girl who spent time thinking about it. So when Jim and I eloped at an all-inclusive couples resort on the island of Jamaica, that made financial sense. My mom had just passed, so I wasn't up for a big party. But I soon realized, walking down the aisle in Jamaica, how terribly I missed my dad, sisters and brothers. There was always something missing...

My first wedding to Mary in California was funny and

joyous, but meager. We found a church on the Peninsula, south of San Francisco, that we loved because of its beautiful stained glass altar. The reverend insisted we be interviewed prior to the big day. When he asked Mary "what is your personal relationship with Jesus?" her eyes widened, and she quickly punted. "Scott, why don't you handle this one, honey?" Come on. "Well, to be honest, I haven't really met Jesus. I try to live my life in accordance with some of his rules. That's it." The reverend wasn't pleased, but the wedding went off without a hitch. We finished at a public park with a blue grass trio and homemade hors d'oeuvres. The celery and peanut butter were to die for. Now, however, 35 years later for me, it was a golden opportunity for a Second Chance Wedding. We were lucky to have an open canvass on which to paint a perfect day. We just hoped the weather wouldn't suck. In May on Long Island, you never know.

The first part of our wedding prep was to learn how to dance. When we first started to date, Scott said he always admired couples of any age who looked great on the dance floor, and seemed to truly enjoy dancing. He wanted us someday to be "that couple." I mentioned a beautiful song that reminded me so much of him called "Open Arms" by Journey, a popular 80's rock band. He loved it. It was a perfect song to waltz to. The song tells about a couple's journey of coming together, then drifting apart, and finally returning to open arms. Scott's open arms embraced me, kept me safe, comforted me, and made me feel at home. A perfect song for us.

I loved Tina's suggestion of "Open Arms" for our First Dance song. I was so inspired by the lyrics, and the idea of dancing like "that couple," that I practically wore her out rehearsing. As we mastered more and more of the 15 part routine, created by James at Arthur Murray in Huntington Station, I would routinely stop the car almost anywhere to practice. Once in a frozen Walmart parking lot next to an idling 18 wheeler, I waltzed her through what we knew thus far. Then it was twirling through the steps at the amphitheater in Central Park. Next it was up and down the sidewalk in front of a Thai restaurant on 10th Street in Manhattan,dodging garbage cans as her sister Toni chuckled in the background. The Naked Cowboy in Times Square got an eye full of our routine when it was nearly perfected. Our 13 inch height difference presented challenges, but where there was a will, there was a way. We waltzed through this eight month prep period on a cloud.

The first time I came into contact with my wedding dress, it was on somebody else! My sister Tonianne, my niece Stephanie and I were in NYC last spring looking at dresses for Steph's wedding in New Zealand. We were enjoying watching Stephanie try on beautiful gowns, and looking lovely in almost all she tried on. One simple but romantic gown caught my eye – and Tonianne's as well. She gave me a playful look and stated "T, if you ever get married again, you should wear that dress. It would look beautiful on you." I laughed. Tonianne was never a fan of Jim, for good reason.

Well, a year and a half later Tonianne and I were in the same dress boutique, and we asked about that dress. We weren't sure if they still carried it. They did. I don't know if I tried on another dress that day. My sister knew me well. It looked beautiful, and I was sold. We love to tell that story.

The idea of a big wedding was not Tina's, it was mine. I wanted to give her and her wonderful family a celebration worthy of them. Tina will tell you she's often surprised at how I want to "live big," and I wonder about that. Most people are rightfully consumed with difficult day to day machinations. My first wife Mary didn't want jewelry or possessions, she wanted experiences. She was in a hurry to see and do it all. "Never let an adventure pass you by," she urged the kids. Maybe she knew her life would be cut short? When she died she was doing what she loved, adventuring. Her sudden passing woke me up too. I always knew the time we have on earth "is not a dress rehearsal." After the tragedy I felt that feeling deep in my bones. If I could make this Second Chance wedding an unforgettable one, I wasn't going to let the chance pass me by.

We were making meal choices, picking the photographer, the music, the agenda for the day. There were so many moving parts, and the wedding planners at the venue seemed so calm. I'm a worrier and a planner. Scott had conveyed to me a week earlier "Tina, it's a choice to perseverate or relax, why don't you quit worrying, relax, and I'll handle it?" So, I took his advice, and relaxed. I noticed him getting shorter and shorter with the venue planners. He was building up to something - "Groomzilla."

When it comes to advice, I'm better at giving than taking. I convinced Tina to let a lot of the worrying go and only focus on enjoying her part of the wedding. "Living Big" creates big expectations for a worrier like me, so when the wedding planners seemed so blasé about our event of a lifetime, something snapped in my head. We had 150 attending, many from out of state. I rented 15 condos for the out of towners at Cliffside Condos nearby in Greenport. Between Tina's bridal party arrival at 9:00am and the end of the party at 10:00pm, there were 13 hours to plan. So many moving parts: music, agendas, arrangements, lodging, etc. I went into hyperdrive. Groomzilla, it was.

The wedding of the century needed a lot of attention to detail. I wanted it perfect. My mom Ellie would have had a ball planning this extravaganza, with her yellow pad lists, coffee and cigarettes. She would have thought of everything. Tina's mom Antoinette would have loved creating the seating charts so her beloved family could enjoy each other, and "supervising" the gourmet cooks at Raphael. They didn't get the chance. I wanted to make them proud.

With the out of town family all arriving Friday and staying close at Cliffside, it was fun to plan the whole weekend. All 70 were invited to the rehearsal dinner right on the Sound at the Soundview Motel restaurant. After a gray rainy week, the wedding weekend dawned perfectly, sunny, breezy and warm. The twenty- and thirty-somethings, two dozen strong, got along famously. Whatever happened that Friday night on the beach in Greenport needs to stay in Greenport. Tina and I have no idea. We went to bed.

I felt fairly confident the night before. The table assignments were all sorted out, my spreadsheets were complete, and everybody made it to their respective condos. The condos were stacked neatly, identical layouts, one above the other in two wings of two different buildings. Tina and I were in #2F, with Dad and Bunny, Dick and Toni in #1F, directly below. Tina's bridesmaids, Becky, sisters Toni and Nancy and niece Stephanie, all had their "spiced wine" dresses and their printed schedules of where they needed to be, and what their role was. My groomsmen, Trevor, John, Dick Summers and Fred Sherman all possessed their marching orders and their navy blazers, khaki slacks and matching spice wine ties. I still had John's jacket and tie in my closet in 2F. I would give them to him Saturday morning. A week before the wedding, I made out and signed the three big Raphael and DJ checks and placed them in the inside pocket of my blazer. Six times that week before the event I checked to make certain the checks were still there - call it superstition. Tina didn't have a wardrobe change during the big day, but I did. I would change out of the blazer and purple tie, and perform the "Open Arms" wedding waltz in my tuxedo pants, bow tie and black vest. A little dramatic effect. So, as I went to bed Friday night in Condo 2F in Greenport, all the ducks were in order. Our 70 closest family were here from California, Minnesota, Florida, Boston, Virginia, even Sweden, and 80 more to arrive tomorrow. I had thought of everything, or so I thought...

CHAPTER 23. The Big Day

It was hard to sleep past 6:00 am the morning of the wedding. We enjoyed the rehearsal dinner on Long Island Sound the night before. I was overwhelmed with feelings of euphoria. All the people I love most in one beautiful room with a magnificent sunset. How could we top that?

We had a full day ahead of us that Saturday May 19, 2012. Stephanie (maid of honor), Tonianne, Nancy, Becky and I were to start at 9:00am in the Bride's Room at Raphael with hair and makeup. Then the ceremony at 4:00pm, followed by a six hour party! We had the Vineyard to ourselves with 150 of our guests.

When I awoke, Scott was gone! That was strange, but I didn't give it too much thought. I needed to take a run on the beach to get my mind and body ready for the big day. I grabbed my phone and noticed there was a text from Jim "wishing me luck." I didn't let the message affect me. I noted it and moved on. I didn't need luck. I had Scott. After my run, I gathered my girls and our belongings and drove over to the vineyard to start the process. Julie and Samantha, the wedding planners, had mimosas and breakfast waiting for us. I had to make a mental note to watch out for the champagne. I had been on a really strict no alcohol no sugar diet for nine months. I wanted to look spectacular in my dress.

My wonderful friend and hairdresser, Kathy, came early to work on all our hair. She brought along a top notch makeup artist who had done my makeup before for special occasions. We were all set.

It's 5:00am, the Big Day. Suddenly I sat bolt upright in the bed, in the dark, in a cold sweat. I forgot my waltz outfit, the pants, the vest and the black shoes!!! Sonofabitch, what a jackass I was! At times like this I revert to anger at myself, but it quickly passes, and I sort my action options. There was only one this time: drive the 90 minutes back to Huntington, grab the gear, and haul my ass back to Greenport. If the Saturday traffic was cooperative, I'd be back by 9:00. I would miss Tina - she had to be at Raphael with her girls by 9 - but in time to take 25 people to breakfast in Greenport. Time to roll. On the road I wondered, wasn't this an auspicious beginning to the wedding of my dreams?

For all our planning, my day had some ups and downs too. I forgot my razor! Luckily Kathy had a clean spare in her gag and decided to help me with my underarm hair. She lifted my arm and started her work. "Ouch!" She got me. Who knew there were veins under our arms? It was a gusher. Blood everywhere. Luckily I was not yet wearing my gown, and the planners had a supply of bandaids. Later there was the makeup malfunction. I wanted fake eyelashes. Scott would love it when we would go to an affair and I put on fake eyelashes. The makeup artist brought her eyelash supply. As she was applying the lashes piece by piece she had a glue malfunction. The fake lash started poking me in the eye! A one-eyed bloody bride! Again, lucky for me my team was equipped and ready to handle all contingencies. They were able to pluck the rogue lash from my eye, stop the tearing, and re-apply the right way. Whew. I was finally ready for my dress.

My girls all wore beautiful simple dresses from J. Crew. All I asked is that they all be in the same color. They all agreed on "spiced wine." They all looked absolutely stunning in this color, and each dress they picked worked beautifully with their bodies.

They helped me put on my simple silk chiffon gown. The dress was everything I felt this wedding spoke about: simple, elegant and romantic. I never understood the "hoopla" about

Beautiful Bridesmaids

weddings, why did ladies get so bent out of shape about this process. I understood at that moment. When the gown was put on and my sisters, Stephanie and Becky looked my way, I felt a special feeling in my heart I cannot explain. I was preparing to walk down the aisle to a man I'd waited for half *my life. He came with three children that I would now help support and love. My family were so head over heals for my new man and how he has brought me into the light, back to them. I often explain my mindset that day was euphoric, like I was floating above myself.*

The wedding planners went to retrieve my dad so he could see me before we walked down the aisle together. When he first saw me, he gasped. I started to cry. This moment was what I was waiting for. The ceremony was about to start.

I pulled into Cliffside by 9:00 having been spared by the Long Island traffic gods, in time to round up our breakfast posse, pour ourselves into six cars and make it to Greenport. I was beginning to decompress from the emergency tuxedo rescue mission, and knew I had only two things to do before I gathered the groomsmen @ 1:30pm to ferry all to Raphael by 2:00: (1)deliver John's navy blazer and spiced wine tie and (2) get myself dressed. Piece of cake. At noon I found John, a little hungover from the beach last night. He looked genuinely excited.

Handsome Groomsmen

Many of his cousins were around. It would be a legendary

day. I handed him the jacket and tie, hugged him, and turned toward my condo. Ah, plenty of time to shower, don my outfit, and meet the boys.

I went to put my key in our condo door, but it was already open. Strange, I thought. I knew I'd locked it. No matter, I thought, overlook it. I walked in, saw my Maui Jim sunglasses on the coffee table, put them in my pocket, and noted, "hmmm, this place is way neater than it was when I left this morning." Tina and I were famous for trashing hotel rooms while we're there. I looked into the bedroom, and standing there, in his underwear, looking puzzled, was my father-in-law, Nick! Holy shit! What's he doing nearly naked in my room? Bam! I realized I was in Condo *1F*, right below my own condo, *2F*. I blurted out "Oops!, see you later!" and scooted out with my tail between my legs.

Wow, that was a shocker! Thanks goodness it wasn't Bunny in the doorway, in her underwear. Whew, time to take a deep breath, shower, and get dressed. The shower calmed me down some. I wore my brown shoes, khaki slacks, white shirt, spiced wine tie, and collected the tuxedo outfit on a hanger for the wonderful waltz wedding dance. Nonchalantly, I reached into the inside pocket of my blazer. No checks. Not one! Here we go again, my heart rate beginning to rise. Now my options were (1) throw myself off the two story balcony, (2) tear apart the condo to find the damn checks, or (3) make embarrassed excuses at Raphael.

#1 looked good at the moment, but I realized the fall wouldn't kill me, the sudden stop would. I chose #2. I ransacked 2F hunting under every couch cushion, in every dresser and kitchen drawer, every cabinet. Of course, no checks. I started to blame the gremlins that occasionally pulled these pranks on me. It was time to meet the guys, so I called off the search. #3 it would be. Humiliating.

In the van to Raphael the four guys were decked out and ready, but Fred said "Scotty, what's wrong? You look like shit!" "You're not going to believe this. I had the checks for the DJ and Raphael written and in an envelope in the inside pocket of my blazer ALL WEEK. I checked on them SIX TIMES. Today, they are GONE. Poof!! Disappeared! I can't believe it! I'm beside myself!" Trevor calmly said "Dad, your blazer is identical to John's right? Is it maybe in *his* pocket?" I said, "No way! I checked!" As Trevor was talking, John reached his hand slowly into his blazer, smiled slyly, and pulled out the envelope. Goddamnit. What was going on today? Relief washed over me -option #3 would not be needed. Dick said "the strangest thing happened today. I left my Maui Jim sunglasses on the condo coffee table, and they disappeared. I couldn't find them anywhere." Now it was my time to solve a mystery by reaching in my jacket. Out popped his Maui Jims, which looked just like mine. I told them the story of grabbing the sunglasses, and walking in on Nick in his underwear. Everybody chortled. I was left to wonder what disaster would hit next? Would I stammer during my wedding dinner speech, trip during the dance, throw up during the toasts? Turned out none of that happened. The wedding would be spectacular. I just needed to realize that when I'm under performance pressure, reality can bend in strange ways!

CHAPTER 24. The Ceremony

Thank God for Samantha, my bridal attendant the day of the wedding, my savior. The walk down the aisle at Raphael started high up on a balcony overlooking the vineyards, continuing down a long flight of stairs. Standing on the balcony, I felt so nervous. When I glanced down at the colorful crowd assembled on the lawn in front of the beautiful trellis, I started to tremble, and tears were ready to flow. Samantha took one look at me and demanded "there's no crying on my watch!" She proceeded to tell me a joke. "What kind of bees give milk?" It was the only joke I knew. "Boobies" I answered, laughing. The tension broken, I was ready to take my once in a lifetime walk to Scott.

The boys and I arrived at Raphael shortly before 2. The place looked spectacular. The bright sun in the vineyards made everything in the winery sparkle, especially the ubiquitous glassware and the glittering chandeliers. We strode, five blazered caballeros, into the massive main hall, where the dancing would take place, and heads turned. We conferred with Father Tom about our places and roles, and chatted with the gathering guests. By 3:30 Julie and her helpers began to herd the 150 guests toward their seats out on the lawn in back by the vineyard. Each aisle seat was graced with a rose. The white flower festooned trellis framed Father Tom as he awaited the initiating music.

A few minutes before 4, the bridal party was assembled by the trellis, everyone grinning in anticipation. Little Eva the flower girl, all dressed up and not happy about it, wove her way halfway down the big aisle with all the people looking at her, and sat down. Mommy came to the rescue, and the crowd laughed a little, relieving the tension. Proud Papa Nick was stationed at the foot of the stately alabaster staircase, awaiting his baby daughter. A hush fell over the crowd. All eyes turned up toward the top of the stairs...

Papa Nick walks his baby girl

I snuck another look onto the lawn where the 150 guests were waiting. I finally understood the meaning behind the phrase "fairy tale wedding.' This was as fairy tale as it gets. I was Snow White, all the Disney princesses wrapped in me. I had to concentrate and snap out of my reverie. Those stairs were treacherous, and my heels were high. I slowly started my descent. The crowd grew silent. I heard a few gasps. When I got to the bottom of the stairs my beaming, handsome, lovable and supportive Father was holding his arm out for me. I took a look at him, and then my gaze went past him to my husband's 100 watt smile that I fell madly in love with at Fat Fish. It's hard for me to describe the walk down the aisle from there. My smile could not have been wider. I glanced at several of my loved ones in the crowd, and their expressions were pure love and happiness. This was the moment we'd all been waiting for - not just Scott and me - but all our loved ones. The rest of the walk I felt I was floating. My feet did not touch the ground.

A few tears of joy

Tina was like an angel wafting down from the heavens, graceful and confident. The entire crowd oohed and ahhed. There were some gasps, but soon a stillness. There were a lot of "little girls" witnessing a dream, and many tears started to well up and spill onto cheeks. At the bottom of the stairs she sought my eyes, which were wet with pride and gratefulness. We winked at each other. Then she turned and hugged her dad. When he turned to guide her down the aisle his smile lit up the crowd. Adding Tina's star light, the walk was dazzling.

My dad gave me the hug of a lifetime, and exchanged some banter with Scott. He jokingly said "I changed my mind, I'm not giving her over," smiled and hugged Scott. My hand passed from my dad's to Scott's.

I took Tina's hand, and it was finally here, the moment I knew would happen even 41 months ago. Everybody we cared about was here, her sisters and my kids were grinning like crazy people. Cousin Rose read The Apache Wedding Song. Sue and Jane read the famous"Desiderata" with gusto. When Sue read the phrase "avoid vexing people," she paused and looked at the crowd guiltily. Giggles. It was time now for the vows.

Since I wrote these vows at Gurneys over seven months ago, I'd looked forward to speaking them to Scott and the world. "I, Tina Marie DeSantis, take you Scott Treadwell Sammis, to be my husband, my best friend and my soul mate. I stand before you along with our wonderful family and closest friends as witness to my promises to you. I promise to love you, respect you, honor and cherish our time together on earth with all that I have in my heart. I promise to stand by your side in good times as well as the hard times, I promise not to run. I promise to take vacation days and to cherish this tremendous gift of a second chance at a lifetime of love and happiness, I promise to let myself be happy. I promise to love and respect your children, my stepchildren. I promise to open my heart and home to them and be there for them in good times as well as the hard times. Scott Sammis, I will love you for the rest of my days with all my heart. I thank the universe for placing you in my path."

How to follow that act? Tina had them all in tears of joy. Her vows were typed up, practiced frequently and delivered flawlessly. Mine are on a crumpled green index card, abbreviated to fit. Here goes: "Tina Marie, I promise forever to honor, adore, cherish and appreciate you, and never to take you for granted. I promise to rub your back, your arms, your neck, your feet (pause) OK that's far enough for right now. Giggles. I promise to meet you at Starbucks *whenever.* I promise to admit to you when I feel vulnerable and sad. And encourage you to do the same. I promise to surface misunderstandings so we can resolve them, never to run, to be patient.

I promise to treat you like the princess you truly are. (Ohhhhhh! from the crowd) I promise to hold you when you are sad, and to laugh with you when you are bratty. I promise to smile whenever I see you. I love you."

Father Tom was gracious and brief, conducting the hands on ceremony and the wine blessing, and soon it was time to kiss the bride. I swooped Tina into my arms, bent her over Hollywood style, and we had a long smooch to delighted catcalls and applause. We are married!! Let the honeymoon begin!

CHAPTER 25. The Celebration

The cocktail hour followed immediately. The photographers and wedding planners miraculously got our families together for what turned out to be amazing photos. Toni, our chief photographer, was a drill sergeant, but she managed to leave no one out.

Scott and I then got whisked away to sample the cocktail hour offerings in a private room. We were too nervous and keyed up to touch most of it. Samantha was in charge of following me around to be certain I had a glass of champagne in my hand at all times. She did!

After the reception line - 150 huge smiles and hugs over 25 minutes - and the precision herding of the two families to immortalize the day in photographs, we disappeared for an hour of hors d'oeuvres sampling and wedding couple photographs all over the winery and vineyards. The guest feasted on the sumptious cocktail hour buffet and then were guided to an elegant separate room to their assigned tables. It was an European style wedding. Dancing and dining apart from each other. Our grand entrance was accompanied by a beautiful Cold Play tune and tons of applause. Speeches by my Best Man, Trevor, my best friend Fred and Tina's favorite niece and Bridesmaid Stephanie were greeted with laughter and tears. Trevor spoke conversationally and confidently about my success, our family history, how proud he is, and his views of happiness. I burst with pride. Stephanie repeated what she told Tina about me when we first met; "he's the white Barack Obama." Her family beamed. My conservative stepmother Marge scowled. Steph was heartfelt and touching. It is crystal clear how much she adores Tina. Fred knocked them dead with advice, quotes and anecdotes from our 20+ year history. Now it was our turn. My heart was pounding out of my chest, wondering if the jinx of this morning was going to disrupt this moment.

Scott's Wedding Speech

I removed my jacket, rolled up my sleeves, and took the mike. I had decided to change up the typical wedding routine, to throw the crowd a curveball. I knew the waiters and waitresses were ready to distribute the dinners after my "brief remarks," but I had some things to say. I grabbed Tina to stand up with me. "Wow," was how it started. "All the people in the world we love the most are here with us in this beautiful place. Happiness is in these connections. Thanks to each of you for coming to share our joy, and to support us. I never thought I'd be here. You know you expect to get married, have kids, that's pretty much it. Often Life doesn't turn out that way. You know the phrase 'man plans, and God laughs.' One message tonight is 'there *is* a second chance, a chance for a new chapter.' When Life throws us curveballs and challenges, we need to stay open, trust in the future, and allow a second chance to happen. This is our message of hope.

"We also have a request. We need your help. You can see what's happening out there. It's hard to stay married. Good people are breaking up all the time. Please support us and stay with us. We'll be there for you too."

Then came the wrinkle. Table by table I acknowledged each and every guest, mentioning where they were from, how far they traveled, and why/how they were special to us. How many weddings have you been to where you didn't know the people at your table or the ones nearby? I wanted everyone to know the significance of each of our special guests. They all seemed a little embarrassed at first but then thoroughly enjoyed the attention. By the end, however, I bet those food trays started to feel very heavy for the waiters.

I was worried that my garrulous husband's speeches would drag. But as I watched the faces as they were acknowledged, I got chills. My loved ones felt so important and connected. That was the exact feeling we were going for. How many weddings have you been at where you get the feeling you were invited to fill a table? And then you did not know the person next to you at the table? Scott and I were determined not to have anyone feel left out.

We had carefully selected the food for the evening, and it was presented magnificently. Everyone seemed to enjoy the feast. We did not get a chance , however, as we immediately started to work the room. There have been way too many weddings where the bride and groom are an enigma. I was determined to say hello and acknowledge each and every guest. Most were an important part of how we got here to this place in our lives. The conversations flowed seamlessly. The love in the room was unforgettable.

Tina was a rock star as she worked the Dining Room at Raphael. She was afraid we would get separated, but I stuck by her side as best I could. Even as we went table to table I began to anticipate mistakes in our upcoming big wedding dance. After all, I was the male partner in the dance, so it was my job to lead. The butterflies were whipping my stomach. The dance was a full three minutes with two dozen distinct waltz moves. Could we pull it off? I did notice that every time Tina hugged someone, she was forced to put down her glass of wine or champagne. When the embrace was complete, the ever present Samantha was there to place another glass in her hand. Tina did not finish a single glass of wine that night. She had a hundred sips. By the time we were introduced to waltz to "Open Arms," she was loose and ready.

All 150 guests ringed the 50 foot wide dance floor under the sparkling chandeliers. The many skylights were casting swaths of golden light across the floor. We had practiced one thousand times, each of our moves synchronized with a different verse of the hauntingly beautiful love song. The DJ surprisingly cut off the introduction to the song, so we hurriedly launched into the precisely choreographed waltz two measures late. We looked at each other and silently mouthed "we got this." Despite the butterflies and champagne sips, we executed the dance flawlessly: the pirouettes, the under arm turns, twists, and backwards sashaying. By the time we the song climaxed and we pulled off the final dramatic dip, the room burst into applause and cheers. We did it!!!

Wedding Dance

The dance party was ready to start. The DJ introduced the wedding party and my Dad and step mom Bunny. Finally, Scott and I entered to perform our first Dance. The moment we had been practicing for two nights a week for nine months. I was buzzing from champagne, and was not nervous at all. We floated together through the dance. There were moments of applause when Scott spun me, and cheers when we dipped. Someone filmed the entire waltz on their cell phone and uploaded it to Youtube. I love to go back to it from time to time. It was a priceless moment. When we finished with Scott spinning me into the grand finale dip, my sisters came running up to us with hugs and sobs. I was never so happy.

The crowd was invited by the DJ onto the dance floor. I don't believe anyone stopped dancing for the next hour or two other than to get another drink.

After the waltz everyone hustled, free styled, hip hopped and tried their hand at Lindy and Rumba. Then it was time for cake cutting and the Father-Daughter dances. The dance floor was hushed when Tina and her proud daddy Nick strode out to the floor. I was expecting them to foxtrot to "Someday" by

Bride and Daddy dance

Frank Sinatra, but the DJ decided to substitute "Summer Breeze." No matter, there wasn't a dry eye in the house as Tina and Nick beamed at each other and glided through the

their turns. Then it was time for Becky and me to swirl through Louis Armstrong's touching "Wonderful World." She was radiant, I was a mess inside. A million emotions coursed through me. I forgot to lead, so we just mushed through. My little girl and her daddy. What a moment. Then the craziness broke out, and we were swept up.

Dad and daughter dance

Around 9pm with the wedding dancing in full reverie, Samantha came and grabbed Tina and me by the elbow, escorting us to where the wedding trellis was. It was now decked out in candles, and two chairs were set at a banquet table. There were two glasses of champagne and samples of all twenty desserts that our guests had enjoyed. We linked arms to toast. The photographer's flash popped over and over, until we saw stars. Remember, Tina had starved herself for at least four months prior to the wedding - no bread, sugar, alcohol, and vastly reduced carbs - to look fabulous in her stunning ivory wedding gown. Now, however, we were married. All bets were off! We dug in. We had essentially skipped dinner, but we did not miss dessert. There were bites missing from every one of the little pies, cakes, torts, cookies, etc. What a sugar rush!

Dessert Splurge

We left our little romantic dessert rendezvous buzzing with a serious alcohol and sugar rush to join our loved ones back on the dance floor. The place was alive with lots of groups. By the end of the night I had danced with every group, laughing and crying with all my loved ones. I was a sweaty "hot mess." The DJ provoked the crowd into tribal exultation with the pounding beats of familiar dance music. I didn't want it to end.

At 10pm the DJ stopped the music, and the air went out of the party balloon. After one more hug and "goodbye," the wedding planners guided the guests to the front to receive their wedding gift - a bottle of Raphael Winery's best - and on to their cars. Trolleys were loading up to take the extended family back to the Cliffside, where the party would continue on the beach. It seemed to me the party was over way too fast. As the guests were streaming out, I found my sister Tonianne in the bridal suite, and we cried and hugged. We were both just a little buzzed from champagne and emotional overload. Scott found us, helped us gather our belongings, and loaded us into the limo to return to the condos. The remainder of the night is a bit blurry for me. I hear I was quite the lady?

The last half hour of carousing is a blur to me still. Not even the older folks sat down. Everybody wanted a piece of Tina and me. The Sammis cousins even picked Tina off the ground and held her horizontally for a picture. We were pulled in a dozen directions, smiling and laughing until it hurt. So much energy and joy. Then, as furious and frantic as the dancing action was, at 10 on the dot, it was over. The DJ stopped, and started to pack up. We hugged everyone who was still standing, sweating, but it wasn't sad. We would see most of them tomorrow. I thanked and tipped the DJ and maitre'd, and went to find Tina. She was back in the Bride's

Room dissolved in tears of happiness, exhaustion, sadness, alcohol and sugar with her sister Toni. The tears made them look like raccoons. I knew I needed to shepherd them back to the Cliffside. Dick and I persuaded a security guard at Raphael to get us four merrymakers back to our condos. Word was the party was to continue with a bonfire down at the Cliffside beach. As we stumbled out of the car at Condo 2F, Tina blurted out "I wanna go to the beach!" I said, "Let's go get changed first, honey."

I followed Tina into the bedroom and began to change out my tuxedo vest and pants for blue jeans and a hoodie. Tina went into the kitchenette. The next sound I heard was beeping noises and swearing coming from there. Peering around the corner I witnessed Tina mashing the buttons on the microwave oven trying to re-heat coffee from this morning. Failing at that, she face planted in the basket of pastries and muffins Tonianne had provided for all the families in the condos. I gently tried to back her off the goodies, but she snarled at me like a hungry bear. I decided I didn't want to lose a finger, getting between Tina and the goodies. In between bites, I tried to distract her, like a rodeo clown waving a red flag at a bull. "Tina, let's open some of the envelopes and cards. Over here, on the couch." Her eyes widened, she refocused, dropped the gluten free blueberry muffin, crumbs on her cheeks, and plopped down on the couch to tear open envelopes. That exercise lasted abut 30 seconds before her eyes rolled back, shoulders slumped, and she succumbed to the exhaustion, excitement, sugar and alcohol. I carried my beautiful comatose bride into the bedroom, wedding dress, hair and makeup all more or less in place. She was snoring instantly. We didn't make it to the beach party. But, I thought, it was a perfect close to our fairytale BIG DAY.

CHAPTER 26. The Morning After

All the carousing, dancing, intense connecting with all of her closest loved ones, champagne, dessert and Toni's goodies all landed on Tina that night of her wedding. I was only a little better. I awoke first. There she was, crumpled into an ivory pile with her eyelashes on her cheeks, mascara raccooning her eyes, hair a bird's nest of bobby pins, blinking at me and scowling, afflicted with nausea. Hardly a blushing bride, but I thought she was the most beautiful woman I'd ever seen. We somehow managed to shuffle her into the shower, minus the wedding dress, and slowly she started to feel human again.

By 9am, on schedule, we're downstairs organizing transportation to downtown Greenport for a cozy post wedding breakfast for 46. When we arrived there were four seats available in the diner that seats only 61. After a brief panic, some tables opened up, more guests arrived, more tables became available, and we took over the joint. Not exactly raucous, considering the ocean of wine and cocktails that were consumed last night, but warm and fun. The owner was happy with the $100 tip. Then we meandered around lovely quaint Greenport before returning to Cliffside. I think none of the remaining 46 close family were looking forward to the goodbyes that morning. We all had such a full, fun weekend. It was a wedding for the ages.

CHAPTER 27. The 40 Year Honeymoon Begins!

Our Second Chance Forty Year Honeymoon started with an eclectic actual honeymoon in my old CA favorite city San Francisco, and then Maui and Kauai in Hawaii. I had spent my first two years after college in SF as a starving job seeker with a BA in History in the City by the Bay, and was anxious to show Tina some of the sights, this time with more than $3 in my pocket. We stayed at the well worn but charming Hotel Beresford Arms on Post and Bush Streets. Very foggy when we got in. Naturally, we started the visit with a walk across the completely encased Golden Gate Bridge, ghostly in the gray soup. The next two days we walked everywhere in the clearing weather, up and down the steep hills, riding the cable cars, enjoying Irish Coffee at Buena Vista Cafe, lunching at House in North Beach, dining at Neptune's and Scoma's on Fisherman's Wharf. We toured the Marina District on segways battling strong winds, but loving every moment. Our last CA day we drove the rental car up to delightful Point Reyes where Shirley Sigmond, Mary's sister, has a cool house. We strolled the beach at the National Seashore, again into a gale force wind. At least it was sunny. On the ride home we stopped at the Gloria Ferrer Winery in Sonoma. A bottle of sparkling rose, a reprise of the wedding waltz in an empty parking lot, watched only by the manager's white lab retriever Oscar, and we were heading back to SF to prepare for the flight to Maui.

Segwaying in SF

We left mid-day Thursday the 24th from SFO to Seattle, then after a long layover, to Maui. This was the only flight we could get when I booked it months ago. We arrived in Maui at 8:30, located our rental car, and made it to the hotel by 10pm. I had booked us a sunrise bike ride down spectacular Haleakala volcano and we had to catch a 2:30am shuttle to the bike outfitter who would ferry us up to the 10,000 foot summit in time to see the mind blowing sunrise. We tossed and turned for 3 hours and then blearily found the shuttle. When I told Tina to bring a winter coat, she laughed at me, but atop Haleakala at the end of May, in forty degrees and 30 miles per hour wind, she was happy to have it. After the sun exploded over the eastern horizon, we joined the group of 10 bikers and wound our way down the mountain for a few hours.

Coolest thing I ever did!

Biking down Haleakala

The day was only just starting to get cool, it turns out. We returned to the hotel for a one hour nap, then it was off to the Harley rental office, where I had scored an 800 pound Road King for the day. I'm used to the more comfortable

Softtail model, and found the Road King heavy and shaky, but familiar. I got less uncomfortable as we headed up north to the beautiful NW coast of Maui. I wanted to show Tina the incredible sparkling ocean waters in the sunset. We made it to the crossroads between Haleakala and the north volcano and I stopped at a stop sign, noticing how windy it had become. Tina was on behind me hanging on for dear life. Turns out the funneling effect of the two volcanoes makes this spot on Maui the second windiest place on Planet Earth. Hmmm. Next thing I knew, a strong gust came up from behind us and blew the windshield off the Road King. Whoa. Need to be a little more vigilant on this ride.

An hour later we pounded our way up to the La Haina area NW coast of Maui, and instead of the sunny spectacle I had hoped for Tina, the clouds had intervened. We stopped a few times, and I grumbled. Tina started to react grumpily to my bad mood. It dawned on neither of us that we were severely sleep deprived. A cute coastal restaurant beckoned to us at about 5 so we stopped. Despite there being two tables by the window, the hostess seated us at the bar. Behind the bar was an attentive bartender who I thought looked a lot like Tina's ex. She smiled sweetly at the guy, and ordered a drink. "This wine is soooo delicious," she cooed at him. He actually didn't pay her that much mind, but I still did not enjoy my dinner. By the time we remounted the Road King, we were in full spat mode. After having her arms wrapped tightly around me all afternoon, now she was arms straight down. I turned and said "come on, this is our honeymoon, we're not doing this." Her arms circled me again.

Before we could go back to the hotel room to crash, we needed to find a deli for milk and Splenda for our morning coffee fix. As I turned slowly around a parking lot, we spied a bride and groom all dressed up. Tina yelled out from the back of the bike,"Don't Do It!!!" and smacked me playfully on the side of my helmet. True to form we got back in the room, ready to fall fast asleep, admitted our fears and feelings, and went to sleep happy honeymooners again.

The next day, Saturday we rode the Road King down the southeast coast of Maui, the Road to Hana. As sunny and dry as the west coast is, the east coast of Maui is a near rain forest, certainly not ideal for motorcycles. Rain on and off, we stopped frequently, hiked and explored some rocky beaches. Lovely, exhausting day.

Sunday it began to dawn on me I may have overbooked this honeymoon. I just wanted to show Tina everything. We got up early to go snorkeling on a huge party catamaran our of Maaleaa Harbor, which I now realized is the second windiest harbor in the world (the windiest is Wellington in New Zealand). As we lurched across the harbor, Tina and I stumbled across the deck for coffee, the ship bucking and heaving, Tina's face got grayer and grayer. We tried on life vests, tubes and swimmies, and she decided to wear them all. When we dropped anchor an hour later, there were whitecaps on the harbor, not perfect for snorkeling, even for an expert, which Tina was not. We were the last ones off the stern platform. And the first ones back. Oops. She was a trooper.

Monday we flew to Kauai, the Garden Island, where the first Jurassic Park was filmed. We stayed at the incomparable Princeville Hotel, on the east coast, on the way to the Na'Pali coast. Room 316 boasted a full view of Hanalei Bay. We spent a busy first day exploring visiting the gorgeous beach. For Tina's birthday, the 29th, we took a Blue Hawaii helicopter tour over the entire island of Kauai. Tina was nauseous at first, but finished the trip gawking at the spectacular cliffs and waterfalls. We flew over the Okalai swamp rain forest which gets 450 inches of rain a year, the wettest place on earth. Tina was thrilled for the helicopter adventure, but equally thrilled to get off that bird. We dined for her 47th birthday at a magical little sunset restaurant.

Helicopter Hawaii

One more day to hike the daunting but exquisite Na Pali coast walking trail, try paddle boarding in the Hawaiian surf (Tina stood up, I pitched over several times and retired), luxuriate on the Princeville Hotel beach, dine in paradise, and enjoy a last sunset. Next day, it's so long to the very first chapter of our Second Chance Forty Year Honeymoon. We really did not want this fairytale week to come to a close. Then we smiled at each other, our signature Bakery Face smile, and took a deep breath. We have another 39 years and 353 days together to look forward to. Thanks to some perseverance, a few good choices, a lot of learning experiences along the broken road, some great advice, and a ton of support from all those who helped us get married at Raphael Winery on May 19, 2012. We are so grateful for our Second Chance, and for the start of our Forty Year Honeymoon.

Happy Birthday in Hawaii

A Final Word or Two

If you find yourself on the broken road, don't lose heart. Prepare, evaluate yourself, figure out what you want in a partner, and try to make yourself into that perfect partner. Don't lose hope. Be ready. You never know when that Someone will walk into your office, or into that sunny restaurant, to change your life, open up your second chance for your own 40 year honeymoon. What's that enticing smell? Why is a smile creeping onto your lips and crinkling your eyes? Quick, find a mirror. It's your Bakery Face!

And, if you are on the path to marriage, either your first or a later chance at that second honeymoon, we encourage you to invest in your story. Slow down and pay attention to all the little details, gestures, thoughts and words you are experiencing. This is YOUR STORY. You will undoubtedly be asked to tell it numerous times. Make it good. Make it juicy. Don't leave out the tough parts. Take some notes so you can remember. Your story will be a gift to all of your family and friends, old and new. And it will be a gift to yourselves, making your marriage even more vibrant and strong. Here's to YOUR 40 year honeymoon!

Prologue

We invite you into our conversation about an unexpected and unique journey we took together over a thirty month period in the middle of our lives. We were both stuck, rattled and rolled into a sense of acceptance of our different circumstances. We had been dealt some hard cards, but life was good. Good enough. Little did we know, a chance meeting on December 8, 2008 would change our lives forever. And provide us a chance for a second honeymoon neither of us dared to hope for. What follows is the wonder, hope, disappointment, surprises and thrills from BOTH of our perspectives.

We hope our story will inspire you to dare to hope.

About the Authors

Tina and Scott are both grateful for successful careers in the Property Casualty Insurance Industry, on the agency side of the business. Tina now owns and operates Better Choices Fitness, LLC, an innovative personal training business, and teaches numerous classes at the local YMCA. Scott is semi-retired, but stays busy with a small businesses teaching kids to code and promoting local businesses on a hyper local social media website. And they're both in love with their two new granddaughters Maryl and Esme Lou.